MW01178635

We don't need more, we need different

Working across organisational
boundaries to solve 21st century
problems

Andrew Hollo

WORKWELL CONSULTING

Copyright © 2012

Workwell Consulting

www.workwell.com.au
110 Gertrude St
Fitzroy VIC 3065
Australia

All rights reserved, including the right to reproduce this book or portions thereof in any form.

Designed by Ned Jamieson.

Cover image: Copyright © 2012 VLADGRIN. Used under license from Shutterstock.com

ISBN 978-0-9874048-0-0

National Library of Australia Cataloguing-in-Publication data is available.

TABLE OF CONTENTS

ABOUT THE AUTHOR

As Director of Workwell Consulting, Andrew Hollo works with all levels of government, the not-for-profit sector and social enterprises — ranging from multi-billion dollar institutions and service providers with thousands of employees to highly specialised innovation hubs doing ground-breaking work with skeleton budgets and staff. The unifying theme of Workwell's clients is their role in tackling the major national health and social issues of our times.

Andrew studied psychology at the University of Melbourne, trading a prestigious early career in one of the world's largest management consultancies for a less lucrative but more socially-conscious challenge: finding work for disabled jobseekers. He did this in the midst of a global recession that saw national unemployment figures top twelve per cent. As testament to his extraordinary success, Andrew soon became a highly sought after speaker, trainer and 'how to' expert. He built his first consulting practice on the basis of these experiences. In 1999 Andrew founded Workwell Consulting, to help leaders of socially-aware organisations increase their impact via systems-level change.

Andrew has also been a radio broadcaster, a teacher of English in Japan and global traveller in five continents. He lives between Melbourne, Australia and Bali, Indonesia with his wife Kate and young son, Jasper.

ACKNOWLEDGEMENTS

Most of all, thanks to my clients. You know who you are. You are all doing amazing work and your passionate belief that the world can be a better place never fails to inspire me. Many of the ideas in this book started as conversations and sessions with you, and I'm grateful for that. I am in awe of the work that you do, and I'm honoured to play a part in it.

If it's possible to judge a teacher by his students, I also believe that you can judge a student by his teachers. In my case, they are John Grinder and Roger Deaner, who opened my eyes to the patterns inside us all, and Don Beck, Chris Cowan and Natasha Todorovic, who showed me the patterns in society. Gratitude to Alan Weiss for helping me become a better consultant, and to Chad Barr and Alex Goldfayn for helping me to understand that a book doesn't have to be weighty — as long as finds its way into the right hands and has impact.

My assistant Ned Jamieson deserves his own acknowledgement page, but in such a small book we'll have to make do with a sentence — enough to express my deep appreciation of his design, documentation, research and conceptual skills. To Trish Pinto, my editor, who brought sparkle to my writing, and to Dean Mason, who showed me how books should be published in the 21st century, I also owe great thanks.

To thank my wife Kate for her support, understanding and encouragement I could write a whole book and my gratitude would still fall short. And, finally, to my young son Jasper who will inherit the world we're creating by being exceptional at what we do.

This is the century for integrators

Gabriella opened the door. She hugged her coat around herself against a biting wind. It was early one evening in Winter 1969 and she was eight months pregnant. Her little boy was at her side, wide-eyed. Both were surprised to see two police officers standing there. What she learned from them would change their three lives unalterably, immediately, immeasurably.

Her husband wasn't coming home. Ever.

The police told her the story: he was running from work for a tram, the roads were slippery, the light poor. He was hit by an under-aged, unlicensed, speeding driver, in an old car. Died on the spot. Oh, and the driver was drunk. And, by the way, so was your husband. Sorry.

INTRODUCTION

I was only three years old when my father left our lives and I remember just one thing about him. His smell: aftershave and pipe tobacco mixed with the slightly sweet smell of alcohol. But I vividly remember the long years of always being the kid without a dad, staying home every Summer while my schoolmates went on camping trips or to the beach, wearing secondhand school uniforms, and arranging buckets to catch the water dripping through our ceiling when it rained.

Where my father, in 1964, set up his small workshop is now an enormous shopping centre, anchored by an IKEA, an Apple store, a cinema complex and several supermarkets—signs of the steady march of inner-urban gentrification. The tram stop — his tram stop — is now a paragon of modern design: all cement ramps, video displays, steel and glass safety barriers. The road is smooth and wide, the lanes clearly marked; traffic lights brightly signaling permission to turn. The cars passing by mostly have four wheel disc brakes, halogen or xenon lights, airbags, and crumple-zones. The speed limits around here are strictly enforced, and the police set up a booze bus at a nearby corner most weekends. The pubs all have rules about who they'll serve: no underage drinking and no inebriated patrons.

I'd like to think that my father's death was avoidable. Not by

1969 standards, but certainly by those of today[1]. In forty years, we have created a dramatically different world, with different regulations, different driver behaviour, different vehicles and different road design.

How have we done this?

We've *integrated to get a job done.*

To illustrate this concept simply, consider two of the stores in the gleaming shopping centre where once my father's workshop stood: IKEA and Apple. These two companies are close to the pinnacle of early 21st century business success because they have worked out something utterly fundamental about human nature. That is, they are in the business of integrating complex processes and systems to *get a job done.* That job is not to sell apps or computer hardware, can openers or quilts. *The job is to answer problems of existence.*

---

[1] The evidence supports my belief: 1970 was the year of the highest number of road death in Australia, when 1054 people were killed on Victoria's roads (close to 4000 across Australia). 2011 statistics are 333 and 1224 respectively. This is a 12-fold reduction when we remember that there are four times as many cars on the roads today compared to 1970. This dramatic decline is mirrored in other Western countries: in the United States, just in the last ten years, road deaths have declined from 45,000 to 35,000 a year.

In IKEA's case, they're problems like:

- 'We're about to have a child and we want to furnish her bedroom'.
- 'My wife's left me and I need to furnish a sparse bedsit — today'.
- 'I've relocated to a new city to work for a year and I need some basics to set up house'.
- 'I need some decent and cheap storage for all this stuff I've got'.

In Apple's case, they're problems like:

- 'I have thousands of photographs scattered across my computer and my phone and I need to sort them'.
- 'I want to watch my favourite programs wherever I happen to be'.
- 'I need my clients to be able to access information regardless of whether I'm in the office or not'.

You might argue that these are hardly *fundamental* problems of *existence*. What about third world infant mortality, or the decline of faith in Western society, growing income inequality in the United States, or other similarly front-page newsworthy issues? The reality is that we won't ever solve complex health, social or economic issues while we see that they're made up of small, separate elements: the equivalent of IKEA's quilts and can openers.

In the case of road fatalities, what we've done over two generations is recognise the larger problem (people are dying and being injured unnecessarily) and then integrate complex sets of activities that are nevertheless coherent (the car designers and tram stop designers don't work together, but their results combine to create safer travel). Importantly, the mechanics of these are invisible to the end user; the average person doesn't care about road camber or xenon headlight visibility and nor do they need to.

This book is about how we can agree on the addressable problems, integrate complex activities performed by partners or collaborators and make these seamless and invisible to those who benefit. Whether we work in education, healthcare, justice, human services, environmental programs, in government, the private sector, academia or the not-for-profit sector, these are increasingly the way we get jobs done in the 21st century. We need to think in terms of *problems of existence*, just like IKEA and Apple do: 'Our customers need to quickly set up apartments for their mothers-in-law' not 'I need to sell more can openers and quilts'. This is called outcome-directed thinking and it is directly relevant to some of our weightiest 21st century problems.

Let's pause first for a moment of self-congratulation. We have truly transformed ourselves over the course of the last century. Imagine a world without the technologies of grid-level power generation that give all of us lighting, heating, washing facilities; the networked communications by which we can contact each other immediately, any time, any place; or the agricultural innovations that have increased corn yields six-fold in a hundred years and wheat four-fold in fifty years (and caused the cost of our food to plummet)[2]. In public health, think of the deaths prevented in just three areas: vaccination (a century ago smallpox used to kill 1500 people a year in the US alone); workplace safety (in a single year a hundred years ago, 177 steel workers died in Pennsylvania alone; today about a dozen steelworkers die in workplace accidents annually across the United States); and deaths of mothers and infants (a hundred years ago, ten to thirty per cent of babies died before their first birthday, and since then maternal mortality has dropped by an astonishing 99 per cent)[3]. Even our IQ has risen by some three points per decade over the course of the last century[4], and the number of

---

[2] Agricultural productivity statistics are from the Food and Agriculture Organisation (FAO) of the United Nation, quoted in http://en.wikipedia.org/wiki/Agricultural_productivity

[3] Public health statistics in this paragraph are from Centers for Disease Control and Prevention, Atlanta, GA, USA. (http://www.cdc.gov/mmwr/preview/mmwrhtml/00056796.htm)

[4] The Flynn effect see Flynn, J. R. (2007). What is Intelligence?: Beyond the Flynn Effect. Cambridge University Press.

people dying globally in wars is in dramatic decline[5].

How have we done this? Largely in four ways, and often with all four acting together: by regulating, by designing new business models and service forms, through technological advancements, and via education.

Isn't this justifiable cause for celebration?

Yes, but not unreservedly. We also added five billion people to the planet in the last hundred years - and not all of them are living well. Our very prosperity and advancement has created new problems: chronic diseases, income inequality, elderly people with nobody to care for them, young people not in school and not in work, a dramatic spike in mental conditions, overcrowded prisons, and the despoiling of rivers, oceans and land.

This class of dilemmas is known as 'wicked problems'. They have no clear solution, and no single cause. Fixing them often creates new problems. Many depend upon changing societal attitudes and behaviours, en masse. Often, wicked problems are related and even interdependent. The well documented relationships

---

[5] Steven Pinker, Violence Vanquished, Wall Street Journal, September 24, 2011. (http://online.wsj.com/article/SB10001424053111904106704576583203589408180.html)

between poverty, school non-attendance, crime, family violence, and drug use is one example. With wicked problems people can't even agree on the nature of the problem, let alone a practical solution. Most importantly, wicked problems almost never sit within the responsibility of any one organisation, or even any one type of organisation (*.com, *.gov, *.org, *edu).

In the old world, we 'fixed' problems such as deaths from workplace accidents, birthing and infectious diseases by possessing two types of certainty: (i) scientific certainty about a solution and (ii) certain allocation of power by authorising somebody to solve the problem (a regulator, a provider, an industry sector). It was rarely easy, but progress was tangible, the public was largely convinced (or unable to object), and people did as was expected of them, with more faith than we have today in government, the military, the church, science, media and corporations.

Today, we're trying to solve wicked problems in a world where many of these certainties have vanished and nobody seems to be in charge. In particular, three new conditions exist:

1. New problems are more complex because we've largely succeeded in solving old problems;
2. New problems require resources which are distributed, not focused and tightly controlled (in other words,

collaborations, alliances and partnerships); and

3. These partnerships require their members to solve new problems by breaking the limiting mindsets associated with our existing tools.

Let's look at one example of a limiting mindset — our tendency to try to solve new problems with old methods. For example, school classrooms look essentially the same as they always have. Kids sit at desks, are told what to do and what not to do. They are given facts and ideas to learn, memorise and manipulate. After all, universal schooling is an invention of the 19th century, intended as a taxpayer funded mechanism to generate the inter-changeable factory personnel demanded by the industrial revolution. Even the long Summer vacation was originally to release labour for the harvests.

In this model obedience and order are rewarded, and deviance and non-traditional approaches are thwarted. Emphasis on testing as the be-all-and-end-all goal means that seemingly superfluous areas — art, drama, music, recess — in some schools are removed entirely to devote more time teaching what will be on the test.

Yet this is at odds with the realities of the 21st century, with its tremendous personalisation (just think of the coffee varieties you can buy) and super-connectedness (think Facebook), its hyper-standardisation (think of the way buildings are made out of components, which are made of components, and so on), its de-materialisation (more and more services for which we pay a *lot* of money don't exist in solid form; things like entertainment, information, financial services), de-localisation (it matters less and less where you live, whether you're buying from Amazon, or trying to get together a support group for sufferers of a rare medical condition). Then there's the increase in time-shifting, via new forms of communication enabled by new technologies, such as video streaming, on-line forums, and social networking, which mean that we do longer need to be in the same place, or even at the same time

If we conceive that the purpose of education is to develop socially and economically capable future citizens - as opposed to test passing, score average raising, and prestige enhancement via the old school ties - then we want a system that is different to the bulk of today's schooling. To achieve this end, we could build those under-recognised meta-skills that are greater predictors of success than test scores or IQ results, for example, the ability to manage one's emotional state, or basic financial literacy. We could give kids outcomes to achieve — building a digital music player for example, and not pieces of activity to perform. We could reduce the reliance on individual scores, recognising that much of what happens in the 'real' world is increasingly collaborative and team-based.

If we're to make these sorts of leaps, together with our partners, we can't just do more of the same. We require both changed thinking and changed action and we need tools and techniques to do this collectively. Sometimes achieving this changed thinking and action is enormously difficult. In my consulting work, I've seen many situations where partners:

- are not always well intentioned towards each other;
- aren't always skilled at (or temperamentally inclined towards) agreement;
- get dragged 'back inside the square' of conventional thought;
- don't always have similar intellectual capacity, or equal knowledge about an issue;
- aren't always coming from a similar values base.

Today, especially if you're a leader, strategist, planner and/ or manager of disparate, multidisciplinary teams, attempts to cut through these sorts of problems will be aided by a cogent understanding of three key factors:

1. Everything's converging. Nothing is staying unconnected in neat parcels or categories.
2. Most of the simple problems have been solved. Only the difficult ones remain.
3. People have higher expectations than ever. They expect user-friendliness, flexibility and fluidity. They expect a computer

that 'just works', or a trip home that won't risk getting you killed.

Yet our tendency to solve new problems with old technologies has created a cult of 'more'. Open a daily newspaper in any city in the world, and you'll see the same tired headlines, calling for more: more justice, more money, better processes, more people, more quality, more innovation. It's usually politicians' or the government's fault, but sometimes corporations', and occasionally the average person's.

I have been a consultant to government and non-profits for twenty years and I have lost count of the number of times I've heard the following prescriptions for a variety of social ills:

- 'Our policy will provide for higher quality services'.
- 'This region needs more investment and resources'.
- 'Consumers expect greater professionalism'.
- 'We demand greater accountability through more measurement and reporting'.
- 'Organisations require more effective change management'.
- 'If we're to truly succeed, we require more innovation'.

You heard it: more, more and more. Please.

As a less experienced consultant, I worked on projects for

organisations with these precise headlines, and underlying set of beliefs around the nature of the problem, and the solution. I attempted to fix ills with these prescriptions, sometimes even with modest success, although it was usually pretty piecemeal. My observation of innumerable government departments, non-profits, corporations and academic institutions with whom I've worked — each and every one of them intent on doing good work — is that some manage to do so while others fail abjectly. What's the difference between those who succeed and those who fail?

It isn't about doing more, it's doing it differently.

My most successful clients do two things to escape the lure of 'more'. First, they adopt new mindsets or worldviews that enable them to *see a complex issue in a different way*. This allows them to address the core truth of the problem. For example, getting people to doctors isn't about more doctors, it's about better triage. Second, they *use what's there* — real, tangible, human motive force and action — by directing groups' and individuals' intention and attention differently. For example, the patients, the doctors and the technology are all there — what is actually required is their coherent harnessing.

So, there you have it. Thought and energy, both done differently. Thinking and acting differently in an *outcome-*

directed way creates three astonishing benefits. For organisations in a competitive operating environment (like IKEA or Apple) it *protects them from being copied*. There's nothing secret about their business models, yet nobody can tie together the complex yet coherent design, supply chain and marketing skills in the same way. For organisations striving to create social value, it enables more people to be involved in co-creating products and services that matter to them because *we care less about who owns a result*. For partnerships that are bringing several sets of unique intellectual property and resources to the table, this way of thinking and acting doesn't just help people see where improvement is possible, but it helps them *how to see*.

In this book, I propose that thinking differently involves *three shifts in mindset*. These mindset shifts are the subject of Part 1. They are particularly relevant in efforts to help groups within complex societies address wicked problems[6]. In these cases what

---

[6] Some examples of wicked problems for which the discussion in this book is particularly well-suited are areas like health (chronic physical conditions like diabetes, expensive and high intervention episodic conditions like cancer, social/mental health conditions), ageing (achieving a dignified independence in old age, palliative care and end-of-life support), disability (including and integrating people in society), social coping (addictions, family violence), liveable communities (public infrastructure planning, community development, economic participation, migrant and indigenous groups), environment (resource efficiency, emissions impact),

works is to:

1. think differently **about what matters**, in particular:
*   use *effectiveness* as our main driver, specifically by using *21st century tools to solve 21st century problems*. For example, in Vancouver, providing drug injecting rooms (rather than hospitals or gaols) has prevented hundreds of deaths;
*   mobilising *those who care most about an issue*, by dramatically magnifying relevance. For example, litter has almost vanished from Australian urban streets because enough people cared about 'tidy towns' (though we're yet to achieve the same result with inner-urban graffiti).

2. think differently **about our end-games**, or outcomes, in particular:
*   know how to investigate and *agree not on cost, but on value*. For example Chilean public housing authorities recognise that people don't *need* a complete house, but a starter kit for a house in the midst of a viable community. This single insight has saved literally millions of dollars;
*   work out *what's really worth measuring*. For example we know that a child who leaves school at Year 10 is 17 times more likely to commit a crime than a child who graduates

---

education (child care and child development, academic performance and retention) and justice (crime prevention, punishment, remediation and rehabilitation).

from high school, so why wouldn't we build educational metrics into our crime prevention measures?

3. think differently **about the two greatest resources we possess**, money and power:
- amplify the return on the money we spend. For example, spending $20,000 on educating elderly people's carers about when to call a doctor may have a better yield than employing a single extra doctor at ten times the cost;
- voluntarily transfer power from ourselves (as planners and providers) to our clients. For example, homeless migrants have a higher rate of home ownership when they are mentored by ex-migrants from their own communities, rather than supported by agencies.

The reason we don't arrive at these sorts of solutions is because our usual method of solving a complex problem is flawed. The wrong question is asked, and it's usually this:

'How can we improve our services, our processes or our results?'

When we do that, we usually proceed in the following way:

- we ask people what they think about the services they receive
- we try to improve individual agencies' offerings based on

these findings
- we then attempt to address co-ordination failures amongst agencies on behalf of people who use multiple parts of the system
- we attempt to strengthen trust and collaboration amongst agencies who have identified that they need to work together better on systems improvements
- as agencies talk, patterns emerge and people start talking about repeated instances of common issues which should be addressed collectively by better joint planning
- eventually, people realise the 'big picture' outcome that everyone's really working towards

Like me, you've probably played a part in one or all of these elements. The seductive dilemma here is that each of these steps can be 'projectised', or carried out separately. And they often are. An organisation will spend $50,000 on evaluating consumer reactions to its services. Or a government will invest $100,000 in 'partnership capacity building' or five (or fifty or five hundred) million on a new program. These disconnected activities can only succeed at a very marginal level and, in their traditional guise, they usually look something like this:

- do your best to represent as many interests as possible
- keep working within existing resources and structures
- latch onto some innovation formula that offers a new idea

- get change managers involved in designing a process

An example of this is a child development program I know of, aimed at 'supporting vulnerable low income single parents', funded by government but rolled out through non-profit service providers. The new idea was a playgroup format for teaching life skills to mothers and pre-school age children. The change managers designed processes for funding, targeting, selecting, training, engaging, recording and evaluating. The providers tried to include every form of vulnerable person they could find — Indigenous, alcohol and drug users, people with mental health problems, recently separated parents, transient or homeless parents. They rolled out the program in its silo. They never connected it with doctors, schools, banks, housing services or psychologists. Needless to say, the groups started well, but between Weeks 7 and 14, most groups had shrunk to non-viable numbers. This was a classic case of leading with program methodology, that is, that 'the evidence tells us that peer-to-peer support is effective'. The problem was that it didn't address the *right* need, and didn't bring enough partners together with a common goal that would *actually make a difference.*

What I propose instead is a very simple thing: turn the direction of the whole cycle around completely, so that you start with a big picture outcome-orientation. If you do this, the steps become:

1. create a shared understanding of the nature of the problem
2. ignite a powerful initial relevance spark to mobilise as many people as possible
3. add the right amount of value (know when to stop value-adding)
4. agree to measure what matters the most (and little else)
5. plan to buy outcomes, not activity or improvements
6. propose a model in which the impact occurs when providers let go of their power

It's only once these six mindset shifts have been skillfully broached, openly debated and allowed to leave their mark that the actual work of design and planning can truly begin.

The practicalities of design and planning for exceptional outcomes in complex environments is the subject of Part 2. Here, we go beyond mindset shifts, to *action*: six things that all successful large-group enterprises do to get outstanding results, even when:

- no single partner has authority over the others
- there are many individual motivations and even power plays
- you don't have the right partners at the table
- some parties are pushing for an unrealistic 'everything for everyone' approach
- you don't have enough good ideas, or the best ideas fall flat

- partners don't all commit to the work they'd said they'd do
- change is resisted or even actively sabotaged, or people have change fatigue

In Part 2, I present two principles that are often at odds with more commonplace approaches. First, *people have a natural capacity for insight and a desire to succeed.* This is a hugely powerful motivating force. Second, groups have resources, people and structures that are already established and with *energy that just needs redirecting.* Use this existing momentum — it's easier to nudge the tiller than to turn the ship around.

1. People have a natural capacity for insight and a desire to succeed. Use this motive force in its raw, natural form by building governance and decision-making systems which recognise that:
   a. people want a *higher-order goal, meaning and purpose* to their activities
   b. success is less about innovation and 'thinking outside the box' and more about having *insights that can be acted upon*
   c. getting people to embrace new ways is not about the management of change, but about *positioning people for success* by increasing their change-readiness

2. In all likelihood there are already actions underway that have resources attached, and for which buy-in has already been achieved. Use this existing momentum to hone and sharpen agreement on which classes of action are worthwhile by agreeing that:

   a. effectiveness comes not from trying to represent everyone, but about finding out *what need is actually addressable*. People love a result even more than they like being heard!

   b. success increases exponentially if you 'act in many ways' by having the *right group of contributors* and knowing exactly how to influence them;

   c. you are neither in competition, nor in silos, but understand that *your outputs are interdependent*, in other words, one of you can't succeed without the others.

In summation, I distill five of the most powerful ways you can help partnerships and collaborations solve their most pressing problems:

1. think differently about what matters (relevance)
2. think differently about what you want (your outcomes)
3. think differently about how you apply your resources (money and power)
4. use latent motive force in people (our natural capacity for insight and desire to succeed)

5. use existing momentum in your groups (combine what already works in different ways)

Entire books have been written about each of the ideas I've raised here. I could have done that too. But just as you don't have time to read most of those books, I don't have time to write them[7]. So here's a summary of my approach, based on tens of thousands of consulting hours with organisations and partnerships that have truly wanted to succeed:

- Of the hundreds of possible high-impact mindsets and actions, I've highlighted just twelve which in my view make the biggest different to collective thought in partnerships and collaborations. With many, I've highlighted a common belief that's so entrenched and accepted that it is rarely questioned.
- I've laid out my argument for each in just a few pages (or a few minutes reading time).
- For each, I've illustrated the core issue with a process visual which is deceptively simple, but upon closer examination, the dimensions/axes/categories mask much deeper and more complex relationships (which are not able to be conveyed in

---

[7] In actual fact, I've made this book as short as possible because I'm tired of those books that present one really good idea, which is usually in chapter one (or even on the cover) and then pad out the rest with examples and stories and diagrams and digressions to enable a publisher to sell a 300 page book.

a book of this size).

- I've summarised each chapter with the major takeaway point, or a few powerful mindset questions. You can use these within your organisation's or partnership's meetings, strategy retreats and the like.

My aim in writing this book is to make working across organisational boundaries perfectly normal. This book is for the policy makers and funders, directors and CEOs, the program and service-level managers who struggle to get people's direction, commitment and action logically aligned and working in unison for maximum effectiveness.

It speaks particularly to circumstances where two conditions exist, namely:

1. when participants are from a variety of organisations, professional backgrounds and values-systems; and
2. when there is no clear authority or authorising framework — in other words, when nobody can pull rank and say, 'Do it this way'

If you're a strategist, a facilitator or collaboration partner, this book will offer you ways to work out what the ultimate objective of your partnership can be or should be, and thereby heighten your own commitment and that of others. It will help you start a range of discussions with your partners, about what you should and shouldn't tackle, about how much 'value add' is enough, and whether what you're proposing should be done by you, or by others, including your clients, patients or constituents.

Most importantly, it will help you respond when other people say that what's needed is more money, more people, more innovation or more change. Of course these things are always useful. But what we need most of all is different thinking and different types of action. This book describes how to do that.

This is the century for integrators, and the time to start is now.

PART 1

THINK DIFFERENTLY

The usual prescription for society's wicked problems is 'more'. But more of the old solutions will only solve more of our old problems. In the 21st century we have more complex and intractable problems than ever before. 'More' won't fix these. We don't need more, we need to think differently in six ways:

- New problems need new tools
- Mobilise the people who care to make change happen
- Recognise real value
- Measure what matters the most
- Spend differently for better results
- Shift power to your clients

1

THINK DIFFERENTLY

New problems need new tools

'You can't solve problems at the level at which they were created'

ALBERT EINSTEIN

Humans are problem-solvers. The stone axe allowed our ancestors to hunt and build. The baby sling freed women's hands so they could forage for food. But every problem solved creates new ones. The axe-wielding, baby-sling toting tribes gathered more food than ever before, but now they had other problems. With better nutrition clans flourished and grew large, and people had to solve the problems of living in groups.

This is the pattern of human progress. Solved problems create new problems and new needs. Continuing to refine old solutions *won't solve new problems. More* or *better* stone axes and baby slings will result in more abundant food, but they won't solve the problem of how to resolve tribal bickering and competition as population pressures mount. In fact, solving the old problem *better* will make the *new problems* even more pronounced.

We see this pattern through to the present day. The 19th and 20th centuries saw stunning and large-scale genius in technological and economic problem-solving — electricity, antibiotics, mass transit, telephony, and flight, to name a very few. After their establishment, however, have you noticed how we seem content to improve upon them only incrementally? If you doubt this, ask yourself whether a visitor from a hundred years ago would recognise most of our social institutions — our hospitals, schools, universities, prisons, libraries or even welfare agencies. I suspect they'd readily identify them as exactly what they are — improved versions of century-old innovations.

I am not for a moment arguing that we should halt incremental improvement. However, I do believe that it's a myth that merely by introducing *more* or *higher quality* products and services, we will solve our most complex problems. Our most intractable (and expensive) problems — chronic illness, school disengagement, drug and mental-health related crime, etcetera — are not going to be solved by incrementally improving 19th century versions of medical clinics, schools or prisons.

To understand why this is the case, and what we can do about it, think about the three 'engines' of progress in the last thousand years. The 'religious engine' of the Middle Ages replaced warring tribes with monotheism and religious doctrine. On these foundations, the 'economic engine' emerged in the 18th century, spreading industrialisation and commerce to all the corners of the globe. This economic engine superbly solved old needs that had been around for millennia: relief from want (for example, mechanisation created cheap food and clothes); authority (police forces and judiciaries protect us from crime); order (dangerous activities like drink driving become regulated); and certainty, with mass production delivering reliable standards. Almost none of these things existed in any measure before the turn of last century and now, a scant hundred or so years later they are commonplace — at least in the affluent West.

The economic engine works brilliantly when corporations, their employees and customers — even the governments of the day — adhere to its dominant paradigms.

Corporations operate as competing entities which provide products and services in a transactional model. Transactions accumulate and translate to cashflow, which provides owners a return on their investment. Their employees are deliverers of products and services, contracted to work under centralised control — the aims of their work, their skills and competencies are harnessed as their employer sees fit. The end consumers of products and services are almost universally passive recipients grouped by market segment who grow accustomed to certain consumer entitlements, which are enforceable by legal (and social) contracts. Underpinning this paradigm are governments, who function as regulators, purchasers and deliverers of a variety of services. These nearly always have explicit targets and provide their funding via some rationed method — appropriations (block funding), activity-based (paying for tasks performed) or capitation (paying per head of target population).

What's wrong with any this? After all, we all depend on these paradigms for order, security, and prosperity.

The answer is absolutely nothing, as long as the problems we're seeking to solve within these paradigms are 20th century problems. These old characteristics are not only useful, but *essential* to the types of institutions which were designed to solve problems of societal order and deprivation. Note that the problems have been couched as *economic* problems, which may be solved by doing 'more' and 'better'. At their worst, such institutions are dizzyingly bureaucratic (think of what it takes to get a building permit or find insurance cover or research a mobile phone plan) and at their best, such systems *can* have a human face (think of our best hospitals or schools).

The achievements of the past

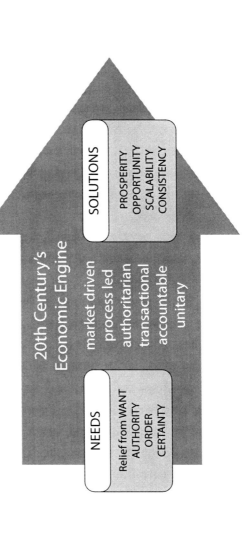

20th Century's Economic Engine

market driven
process led
authoritarian
transactional
accountable
unitary

NEEDS

Relief from WANT
AUTHORITY
ORDER
CERTAINTY

SOLUTIONS

PROSPERITY
OPPORTUNITY
SCALABILITY
CONSISTENCY

Our problem is that we've succeeded in solving our old problems — and now we have new ones. We've solved the problem of lifespan (threescore and ten was once considered to be a long life, yet nowadays a death at seventy is considered to be almost premature) and in its wake, we have new ones: how to live independently and with dignity into one's 80s and 90s, how to manage the chronic diseases that invariably mount up but won't kill us, and how to pay for — and staff — the medical and social care required at end of our lives.

To deal with these infinitely more complex problems of the 21st century, we don't just need more and better doctors, nurses, social workers and aged care accommodation. We need organisations capable of conceiving *and* executing genuinely new approaches to solving problems that are *less economic and more social*. What would such organisations look like? I believe that their defining features are that they'll nearly always be partnerships. And that with their **partners**, they'll **aggregate** and **collectively coordinate self-led approaches** towards **individually determined outcomes**.

I know that's a mouthful, so let me break that down from the perspective of the end-user, client or consumer:

- **Partners**: Very few of my pressing needs (health, education, housing, financial security) can be met by a single organisation. I am supported in all of these by multiple providers: for profit, government, non-profit, and/or community-based.

- **Aggregate**: I want to know that those organisations in whom I place my trust (and give my money) have knowledge of my needs based on their past experience with hundreds, thousands and millions of others like me.

- **Collectively coordinate**: I don't want to purchase lots of little bits of a solution — I want someone to help me plan, navigate and receive a seamless and unbroken experience that works.

- **Self-led approaches**: I don't want to be a passive observer of my own life — I want to understand and take responsibility for decisions and be able to make choices from a range of clear alternatives.

- **Individually-determined outcomes**: I don't want to buy a package off the shelf — I want the organisations I work with to understand my larger goals and customise their offerings to suit my resources, timelines and other supports.

So we don't want higher quality family doctors (well, we do, but not *just* that) — we also need *re-thought* primary health care systems. We don't just need higher quality teachers or curriculum design — we need new ways of *conceiving* learning for the 21st century. We don't need higher quality prisons — we need *new thinking* about natural justice, re-offending, sentencing and rehabilitation.

The 'old' institutions described above (and add to them most retailers, banks and universities) were, and are, static, authoritarian, process-led economic engines. But today, we are moving towards more participative, generative, user-centric 'social engines' — like TED (media/education), Kickstarter (innovation/entrepreneurialism) and Kiva (microfinance/third world development).

These are corporations and non-profits that are increasingly collaborative, and which engage very differently with their communities of users. A case-in-point is 'TED Talks', a magical eighteen minutes in which a leading scientist, researcher, designer, mogul or explorer distills a lifetime's work or presents a powerful point of view. Originally — and still — a conference, TED Talks are now watched 120 million times a year, generating millions of recommendations via Facebook and Twitter. That's substantially more than the online educational content of most American top-shelf universities, combined.

TED's motto is 'ideas worth sharing' and this wide dissemination isn't the only way that user engagement is increased. Anyone can set up a TED event for themselves and in its first year alone, there were more than 600 TEDx conferences globally.

More than 3,000 volunteers have translated 10,000 videos into at least 77 languages, creating a potential audience of over two billion. Social engines such as TED recognise the complexity of their end-users' needs by aggregating these skillfully — setting up specialist TEDs (like TEDMED for health and TedEd for education) and helping participants network. What these delivery methods do superbly is understand that only a part of the value chain is economic; the rest is social.

The way these organisations are structured is also different. Their employees are not operating within a 'delivery' paradigm, but see themselves as designers, enablers and facilitators. A wonderful example of this approach is Kiva, an organisation that offers micro-loans to equally micro Third World business people. Most of its debtors are women, who borrow on average about $400, and use this money to set up spinach farms in Cambodia, run hot dog stands in Nicaragua, do carpentry in Gaza, raise bees in Ghana and sell fish in Uganda, to name just five of Kiva's 850,000 loan recipients. The money comes from people like you or me. We don't get a return on our money, but the money is paid back (in 99% of cases), with interest, to local partners. In this model, 'leaders' are not at the tops of hierarchies, but distributed throughout Kiva's partner organisations — although in many cases, organisation is too strong a word. Networks or ecosystems would be better.

In Kiva's model, consumers are active participants who co-create (sometimes with each other — and sometimes with more formal organisations) because they are empowered to do so. These approaches are particularly powerful when they solve local problems at the lowest level.

Even the role of governments is altered in a world where 'social engines' will become more common. They'll slowly move from roles as owners and funders of services to become catalysts and eco-system builders, bringing about better social, environmental and economic health. Even their funding models will shift towards paying for societal outcomes and they'll be increasingly likely to seek co-contributions from other sectors.

These social engines of the 21st century will largely operate in partnerships that share basic beliefs, namely that:

- the user's outcomes are sacrosanct (not 'service delivery');
- relationships and trust are the new currency (not 'lifetime revenue');
- the user expects our processes to be invisible to them and their experience to be one of ease and simplicity (not 'entitlements' that are then contested and have to be battled for);

Our old solutions won't work for our new needs

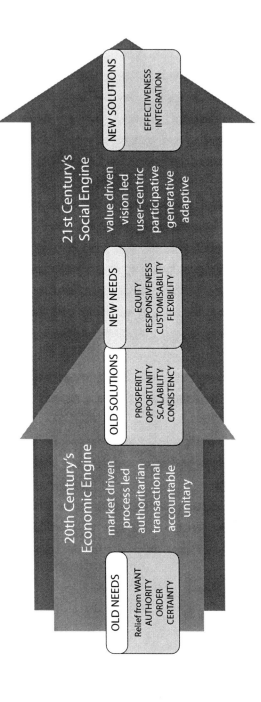

20th Century's Economic Engine

market driven
process led
authoritarian
transactional
accountable
unitary

OLD NEEDS

Relief from WANT
AUTHORITY
ORDER
CERTAINTY

OLD SOLUTIONS

PROSPERITY
OPPORTUNITY
SCALABILITY
CONSISTENCY

NEW NEEDS

EQUITY
RESPONSIVENESS
CUSTOMISABILITY
FLEXIBILITY

21st Century's Social Engine

value driven
vision led
user-centric
participative
generative
adaptive

NEW SOLUTIONS

EFFECTIVENESS
INTEGRATION

- our success is proportional with the number of users who evangelise about us (not our 'market share'); and
- our products and services are best designed in tandem with our users (not exclusively by 'experts')

Our obsession with quantity has helped us solve our 'old problems' of social order and large-scale deprivation. And this is definitely not to be sneezed at. Naturally, *this must continue* but our new work must *build on it*, not just do more of it. This new work, when commonplace amongst partners, will solve our 21st century problems of how to create the sorts of opportunities that people are seeking today: those which are flexible, responsive and customised to our real needs and aspirations.

Key mindset question: Are you solving old problems with old methods, new problems with old methods — or new problems with new methods?

- Are you partnering with genuinely complementary organisations?

- What client experiences can you aggregate?

- How can you collectively coordinate micro-processes to create a seamless experience for your customers/clients?

- How well do you understand the 'big picture' objectives of your clients?

2

Mobilising the people who care to make change happen

'There is nothing more powerful than an idea whose time has come.'

ATTRIBUTED TO VICTOR HUGO

What's the difference between partnerships that bring about sustained change, and those that don't?

The 'Occupy' Movement started near Wall Street in New York in early 2011 and spread rapidly around the globe. In Melbourne, Australia, the banner that acted as an unofficial mission statement read, 'This occupation is a proclamation of solidarity with the millions of people occupying cities around the world right now. They and we seek economic, political and

48

social change that will lead to a more just and equitable society. We are the 99%'.

Why *won't* (or by the time you read this, *hasn't*) the Occupy movement succeed in its aims? There are four very simple reasons:

1. there's not a basic, underlying, simple 'truth' which speaks to the **real experience** of the multitude;
2. they don't have a series of **focused messages** framed as 'what we *do* want';
3. they don't have any **organising principles** (apart from protest);
4. there are no **obvious vehicles** for getting the change they want.

All successful large-scale change meets each of these conditions. Consider two very different social change measures: civil rights in the USA in the 1950s and 60s, and the voting franchise for women in most Western nations between the 1890s and 1920s. Both met each the four conditions above. There were **underlying truths** to which large numbers of people were routinely exposed. Every time a woman applied for a job and was told she'd earn half what a man earns, or every time an African American tried to get on a bus or sit at a diner counter, they confronted an unpalatable truth.

Dramatically heighten relevance

The **focused messages** were clear. In Martin Luther King's 'I have a Dream' speech of 1963, he said, 'I have a dream that my four little children will one day live in a nation where they will not be judged by the color of their skin, but by the content of their character'.

The civil rights movement — which culminated in groundbreaking legislation of 1964 and 1965 — was characterised by the following **organising principles**:

- popular literature on the subject;
- legal cases tested the legitimacy of discriminatory practices;
- musicians established record labels and penned protest songs ('Strange Fruit' by Billie Holliday was about lynching), performing to mass audiences in public facilities;
- Little League Athletics became the first non-segregated sport;
- peaceful 'sit down' strikes occurred across the nation; and
- the 'second great migration' of over five million citizens from states where African Americans couldn't vote to those where they could.

What these phenomena all have in common is decentralised, but mutually-reinforcing purpose, directed not just at those who stood to benefit directly (that is, African Americans) but at all who believed that the status quo was unjust or improper.

Finally, there were obvious **vehicles** to achieve change – most notably legislative change — in the Civil Rights Act of 1964 that banned discrimination, and the Voting Rights Act of 1965 that restored and protected voting rights for all American citizens.

There are numerous case studies across hundreds of important social, economic and environmental causes that illustrate the critical importance of the four factors described here. One example is the provision of universal health care in Australia. The introduction of Medicare almost four decades ago and its continuation in one form or another to this day involves a tacit partnership between governments, health providers, insurers, and pharmaceutical companies. From time to time this partnership falters, and it's often uneasy, generally as a result of resourcing issues. Yet it survives because the four conditions of real experience, focused messages, organising principles and vehicles are met.

As I write, Australia is about to trial a system of universal disability insurance, which will mean that any person who sustains an injury or disability for any reason will have their care and support costs met. This is a major social innovation which for which all four of the conditions described above are present and, again, is a partnership between government, insurers, disability service providers and representative bodies.

Key Mindset Questions:

If you're in the business of social change, whatever its intent, target audience, form or scale, ask yourself:

- How will I get the public to take a powerful interest in this at the basic level of their primary experience?

- What simple, clear positive messages sum up our basic intent - and how can we couch these as viscerally as possible?

- How can we combine as many intersecting and mutually-reinforcing organising principles as possible, by linking academia and the person-on-the-street for example, or the highly organised to the organic; the pre-prepared and the spontaneous?

- What vehicles will give us the change we actually want? For example, is this a tax issue or a funding issue, an organisational issue or policy issue, a legislative issue, or to do with factors of economic or social behaviour?

3 THINK DIFFERENTLY

Recognising real value

'Strive not to be a success, but rather to be of value.'
ALBERT EINSTEIN

The average addict knows all about the law of diminishing returns. That first hit is marvellous, it relaxes, it soothes – it's euphoric. The next one goes down almost as well – it's still pretty wonderful. The third and fourth maintain the feeling nicely. But the fifth and sixth are scarcely noticeable. They're extras that cost money and take time, but don't actually add any value. This is called satiation. It's when we're incapable of taking any more in.

Whether we're talking about drugs, alcohol, shopping, eating, hi-fi equipment, fine wines or cigars, the rule is the same: there's a point at which further investment is not justified by the gain it's going to achieve. The first effective human study of this phenomenon was in agriculture. People thought that their crop yield depended on how many seeds they planted. Every six seeds yielded about five plants. If you planted twelve seeds, would you get ten plants? What if you planted 24 seeds, or 36? Do the same rules apply? Not necessarily. Yes, you might get more plants, but only if the seeds were planted far enough apart, because if your plants are too close together they'll be competing for moisture and light. There'll be winners and losers. This process is called optimisation.

Now imagine a city government with a crumbling old swimming pool. It clearly needs replacing. The city could spend five million dollars refurbishing it, with the end result of an old pool that's been patched up. The state government intervenes, with an offer of twelve million dollars towards the cost of a new pool. But this creates a problem: even if the city already has the land, which it does, twelve million dollars is not almost enough to build a new pool. The city's question becomes: how much is a new pool *worth*? Should it build a twenty million dollar pool, or a forty million dollar one, or one for sixty million? Or maybe the city should build the best pool in the state, the new gold standard in civic pools, a flagship public works project at a cost of a hundred million dollars or more?

What are the considerations here?

1. **Ultimate purpose**: the reason for the existence of city or local government is to increase the liveability of a community. How would the pool do this? Is it more than just a place for kids to go on hot days? Does it help parents who need respite? Does it increase health and fitness? Does it provide elderly and disabled people with forms of therapy? Does it provide social connection for the lonely and isolated? Does it make an otherwise bland and economically disadvantaged part of the city vibrant and exciting? Does it create at least a handful of local jobs?

2. **Opportunity cost:** the city doesn't have money lying around looking for a purpose. To build a pool, it will need to either increase taxes or borrow money — in all likelihood, both. The question now becomes, what *don't* we do now because we've invested in this new pool? Do we defer road maintenance, live with the unreliable heating and cooling in the arts centre, and leave the rundown beach foreshore area the eyesore it's been for years?

3. **Lifespan cost**: With a major initiative such as this, the upfront costs are only part of those that will be incurred throughout the pool's lifespan. So can the pool earn income, not just via swim fees, but through classes, room hire, food

and beverage sales, and/or functions? Sadly, the answer is that a public pool can earn its keep with a decent margin, but rarely pay back the substantial original investment.

4. **Politics**: Who gets the kudos if the pool gets built? Ministers, mayors, or the bureaucrats? The city gets some good press, and perhaps the new pool will win an architectural prize or a liveability award. Governments think in four year timeframes, which is about the time it takes to conceive, plan and build a pool. Potentially then, it's a nice flagship project and cornerstone of a re-election platform.

But here's the real dilemma: we still don't know what the pool is worth. Will a twenty million dollar pool achieve the city's objectives as well as a sixty million dollar pool? And what is the objective? The objective is community support; the community saying 'We would re-elect the people who built the pool' or more specifically, the community saying 'We've got a great leisure facility in our community'. If you spend nothing, the result is zero people saying these things. If you spend five million on the refurbishment, you'd get a small number of people saying these things, but not many. If you spent twenty million, you'll get more again, but you wouldn't get four times as many if you spent eighty. The increment ends up as a curve, not a straight line, as illustrated in the diagram opposite.

Someone has to draw that value curve, or at least estimate it, so that you can place a red dot on the point where the curve shifts its angle from going up, to going sideways. That's the sweet spot.

How do you do this? To find that sweet spot on the value curve, organisations and partnerships and organisations can consider the following questions:

- **desire**: what do your end users want the most? And the least? Most people naturally want a bit of everything, but organisations need to find ways to discover the handful of things about which their constituencies are most passionate, and for which they seek outstanding accomplishments. And those on which they're happy to see the basics delivered.
- **satiation**: at what point does satiation set in? Each type of project will have its own economics. Some are not worth doing cheaply, while others can be scaled from very small seeds indeed.
- **opportunity cost**: what else is rendered unaffordable by each increase of, say one hundred thousand dollars, or one million? What can't be done because this thing is being done?

If you plot the red dot on the value curve correctly, you will have two distinct segments underneath your curve, one on either side of the dot. Below and to the left of the dot is 'what

Determine value not cost

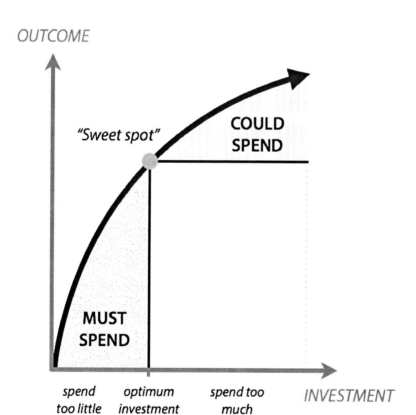

we must do'. This is what your community, constituents or users *expect* you to spend, as their satisfaction (however you measure it) increases disproportionately with each dollar spent. Above the dot is 'what we could do'. This is optional spending which satisfies some needs, but is beyond the point of satiation for most potential users. If you are a publicly accountable body and you miscalculate in either direction, you'll attract the attention of the tabloid press — 'We are being deprived!' or 'Wasteful spending by government!' This is not to say you can't win but, rather, that you need to position that red dot rather carefully.

Key mindset question: For a given project or initiative, how will you calculate the sweet spot, the point at which value, as judged by end-recipients, stops increasing no matter how much money or effort is thrown at it?

Specifically, you want to know:

- How do we establish the value per dollar expended at the level of the end-user?

- What are the consequences of spending too little, and of spending too much?

4

THINK DIFFERENTLY

Measuring what matters the most

'We should measure welfare's success by how many people leave welfare, not by how many are added.'

RONALD REAGAN

I spend part of each year living in Bali, Indonesia. It's true to its stereotypes: swaying palm trees, fluorescent green rice terraces, graceful people, delicious satay eaten from roadside stalls, temples a riot of colour and the sounds of gamelan orchestras crashing out from village pavilions. Then there's the not-so-nice side: roads choked with traffic, the proliferation of Western fast food, bars and convenience stores, tourist throngs… Australians — and others — abroad, living the ugly cliche.

It's a Third World island with First World problems. One of these is litter. Twenty years ago nearly everything on Bali was biodegradeable. Today, discarded bottles, packaging from noodles and biscuits and plastic shopping bags fill gutters, streets, rivers and lay strewn across its beautiful beaches and reefs. There is no proper infrastructure for collecting rubbish, no education for people about littering, and no regulations around packaging or disposal.

Imagine you'd assembled a group of partners to solve this problem. Put aside *how* you'd do it for the moment. What would your measure of success be?

- tons of garbage collected and sent to landfill?
- the cleanliness of reefs, beaches and waterways?
- the ten worst rubbish hotspots cleaned up?
- an increase in the percentage of food/shopping outlets offering biodegradeable containers/bags?
- more villages with at least one communal rubbish collection point?
- more landfills closer to more villages?

More measures allow us to be very specific. Indeed, very thorough. But does thoroughness and detail enable us to miss the point altogether?

The diagram overleaf describes a *tiered* way of thinking about outcomes. I've taken the excellent work my home state is

Measure the right things, at the right logical levels

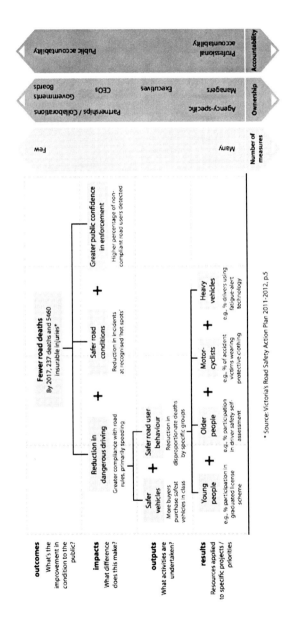

	Number of measures	Ownership	Accountability
	Few	Partnerships / Collaborations	Public accountability
		Governments Boards · CEOs · Executives · Managers	
	Many	Agency-specific	Professional accountability

outcomes
What's the improvement in condition to the public?

Fewer road deaths
By 2017, 237 deaths and 5460 insurable injuries*

impacts
What difference does this make?

Reduction in dangerous driving
Greater compliance with road rules, primarily speeding

+

Safer road conditions
Reduction in incidents at recognised 'hot spots'

+

Greater public confidence in enforcement
Higher percentage of non-compliant road users detected

outputs
What activities are undertaken?

Safer vehicles
More buyers purchase safest vehicles in class

+

Safer road user behaviour
Reduction in disproportionate deaths by specific groups

results
Resources applied to specific projects / priorities

Young people
e.g., % participation in graduated license scheme

+

Older people
e.g., % participation in driver safety self-assessment

+

Motor-cyclists
e.g., % of accident victims wearing protective clothing

+

Heavy vehicles
e.g., % drivers using fatigue-alert technology

* Source: Victoria's Road Safety Action Plan 2011-2012, p.5

doing to make roads, and driving, safer. Victoria, Australia, with a population of five million people, is a world leader in prevention of road deaths, having reduced deaths and serious injuries twelve-fold since their peak in 1970. If you look at the chart opposite, you can see an approach to measurement that classifies four powerful questions into logical levels, which in turn drive different levels of detail in measurement.

Each answers a particular question:

1. **What matters the most?** More people alive and well — or fewer road deaths. This sits at the top of the hierarchy, as the ultimate *outcome*.
2. **What works best?** The evidence around road safety tells us that a combination of driver habits, road design and enforcement delivers optimal results. These become our desired *impacts*.
3. **Where can we rationally invest?** In the area of driver habits, for example, an investment in a major driver-by-driver re-education and re-licensing initiative will be cost prohibitive. But we can focus on the two major areas: the cars people drive, and the protection they afford. We can direct people towards the safest vehicles and target the specific categories of users most likely to die or be injured.
4. **Who/what would bring about the fastest, most positive result?** We will see results most quickly if we target young

people, old people, motorcyclists and truck drivers.

I call this a 'logical levels approach'. It enables us to measure the value and purpose of a given activity. Of course we still want to know *what* to measure within each box. The answer here is simple: *measure that which will create improvements*. There are four ways to do this:

1. **Philosopher's Method** (*framed in terms of outcomes*): 'What would be the result of X?' or 'What is our purpose for doing X?' where X is an activity of some sort. These methods ensure that we're describing ends and not just means.

2. **Optician's method** (*forced choice*): 'Look at this pair of measures: a and b. If you could achieve one and not the other, which would it be?' These methods force prioritisation within finite resources.

3. **Entrepreneur's Method** (*competitive differentiation*): 'Of these measures, on which do you want to be distinctive or even outstanding, and on which are you happy to be merely average?' This method sifts shared views about high performance and forces a reality check on what really needs to be exceptional, as opposed to a default position of 'we want to be good at everything'.

4. **Theologian's Method** (*shared beliefs*): 'Identify five to ten principles for which you agree to held accountable'. Then, invite the challenge: 'How do we prove we're doing these?'

Part of the mindshift required is to always consider and demonstrate how activity relates to results.

My experience with my best clients has taught me five important reality checks:

- Not all results are equal. That doesn't mean 'get rid of some results', but rather demote them. They are of interest to the people delivering a program, but alone they are not of great interest to leaders and strategists.
- Put measurement in the hands of those doing the work, not those of an external compliance agency (this can create adversarial relations). If you're concerned about dishonesty, it's a signal that your measurements are incorrectly focused — they should be about demonstrating value and creating improvements.
- Use publicly visible 'dashboards' that calculate achievement against a handful of the most important outcomes (if children, people with disabilities and accountants can use these, we can too).
- It's OK to measure even if you're not the sole contributor to the result.
- Too many measures equates to meaninglessness: after all, metrics only exist to inform decision-making.

Back to Bali. It has no industry, only enough agriculture to feed itself, and no services sector. The island is almost totally dependent on its 2.5 million tourists who indirectly contribute seventy per cent of the local economy. This in itself provides a powerful argument that the number one goal in efforts to clean up Bali should be *to protect and enhance tourists' experiences of Bali — its roadsides, reefs and beaches.* If your reaction to this is, 'But wait, why are two and a half million tourists more important than four million Balinese?' remember two things. First, that addressing this number one goal will, in its wake, ensure that many smaller things must happen. And, in doing so, many of the measures listed above will then fall into the appropriate logical levels beneath this key goal.

Key mindset question: Are you measuring outcomes that matter the most, or merely your activities and outputs?

Measures ought to answer the question of value and purpose, that is, 'to what end'? Your measurement should always be in pursuit of the incremental achievement of these ends, regardless of (or as well as) what your funders or regulators insist you measure.

Results also support organisational accountability. People's performance is closely tied to their ability to link their individual performance to the bigger picture. This is why logical levels are so powerful: they create ways of understanding organisational effort to the level of the performance of individuals and teams.

5

THINK DIFFERENTLY

Spending differently for better results

'It is not necessary to do extraordinary things to get extraordinary results.'

WARREN BUFFETT

Most calls for 'more', whether it be more hospital beds, teachers or police presume that more hospital beds equals less sick people; that more teachers means more children educated; or that more police equates to more criminals being caught. This is a simplistic, linear view — yet it prevails in organisational thinking. But can we think about the investments we make in complex social problems differently? And how do we do this at a time when overall public spending is flat or declining, community expectations are rising, and the risk appetites of governments and not-for-profit agencies are in decline?

The economist Adam Smith, in 1776, described how pins were then made. He observed that a man working alone could produce at most, twenty pins per day. If you employed two men, you got forty pins, three men, sixty…and so on. This is basic *linear* increase (the dotted line on the chart overleaf). Linear thinking is easy to grasp. It is effective as long as we have funds to increase the number of hospital beds, teachers and police *at the same rate of increase* of serious illness, children in education and crime. Our problem is that *demand is not linear* (the thin grey line). *But we act as if it is*, by funding (and asking for) 'places' for clients, staff 'positions', and patient 'beds'.

Smith then considered what happened if the pin-maker — rather than introducing any major new ideas or innovations — simply *optimised* his existing processes. Instead of a man making an entire pin himself, he divided pin-making into eighteen tasks and trained workers in just one or two. He also equipped them with simple labour-saving devices to straighten and cut wire. He found each man could produce 4,800 pins a day (represented here as the dotted line). With insights such as these, you can see why the industrial revolution was a revolution, not mere evolution, and why the lure of optimisation is so seductive.

When my clients seek to optimise their return on a fixed investment of dollars, people or infrastructure, I advise them to consider the following five factors, in this order:

Three results from three different purchasing approaches

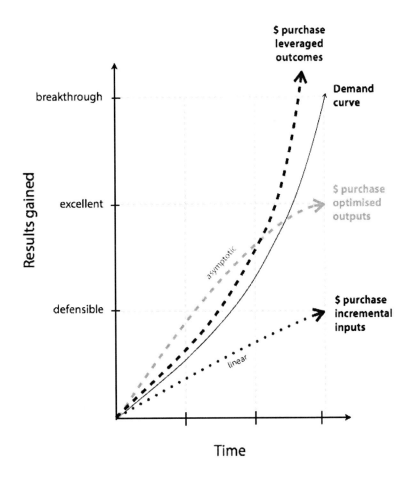

1. musts versus wants — restricting yourself to providing *what really matters*
2. predictors of results — knowing what *contributes to outcomes* and doing more of that
3. division of labour — allocating tasks to the *lowest cost producer* by whom a task can be done
4. process synchronisation — ensuring 'right thing, right time, right place'
5. reducing acceptable waste — eliminating *unnecessary time and effort* that is sometimes accepted as a 'cost of doing business'

These optimising measures will yield the dashed pale grey (asymptotic) curve: you'll see great results at first, giving a great sense of achievement, but there will be less and less advantage over time.

Since Smith's time, we've gone much further than merely optimising. As I write this from my home in Indonesia, in front of me sits a box of Chinese-made pins. With materials, tooling, labour, transport, warehousing, wholesaling and retailing *all included*, the end cost to me is about twenty cents. To have dramatically *leveraged* hands-free mechanisation and modern transport logistics to this point (pun intended) is truly astonishing and would have been inconceivable in Smith's day.

My consulting practice, Workwell, has two types of clients: those who tell me they want to optimise the return on their investment ('We want to get more from each dollar'), and those who want to harness the multipliers of their investment ('The economics of our funding model aren't sound; we need to find ways of leap-frogging our results against each dollar spent'). I usually remind them that they shouldn't be making a choice between just these two, but that they need to think about combining three methods of growth:

- **Linear growth** — which creates scale: the more people/places/hours that you offer, the greater coverage you have and therefore more people who benefit.
- **Optimisation** delivers efficiency — working out what's essential and then examining each essential element to ensure that every dollar and hour is spent well.
- **Leverage** for enhanced competitiveness — remember that every one of your competitors can also optimise and resources permitting, grow in a linear way. But finding your own unique technology, capabilities, partnerships or program designs will position you in a way that others will find difficult to imitate and your funders/grant-givers will find difficult to resist.

The dashed dark grey curve shows how leverage enables you to be ahead of demand. There are several reasons for this. Optimisation has a built-in law of diminishing returns; you eventually exhaust the possibilities for incremental improvement. Linear growth will never keep up, because it delivers more of the same, and always lags behind demand. Leverage enables you to make breakthrough leaps, so its curve is less smooth in reality but in fact a series of jumps and plateaux.

But *how* can an organisation *use* leverage for dramatic breakthrough results? There are two main ways: by *intelligent resource utilisation* and *becoming a catalyst*.

A common example of *intelligent resource utilisation* is a hospital that uses its teaching and research resources to deliver high levels of care across a wide range of conditions. If the hospital attracts a leading urologist, for example, he or she can train others, advise less experienced practitioners, attract research dollars and so on. This far outweighs gains in employing more generalist surgeons, nurses or by optimising surgical procedures.

Becoming a catalyst is when an organisation uses its position to bring together partners who have shared interests or investment in a higher order outcome. *Economic* catalysts for example, add value by facilitating interactions between two or more groups of customers who need each other in some way, such as auction houses and magazines, or credit cards and software platforms. In solving wicked problems, the *social* catalysts are philanthropic trusts, social venture capitalists, research institutions and the like, as well as those who facilitate new partnerships.

The dashed dark grey exponential curve in the diagram demonstrates how leveraging — either by intelligent resource utilisation or by catalysing — uses fixed resources to magnify the outcome by breaking established linear rules. This is usually achieved by acting on one (or more) of the following principles:

- networks are smarter than hierarchies, that is, that co-ordination increases efficiency;
- more are wiser than a few — the wisdom of crowds — the most powerful (and free) resource we have;
- integration is more powerful than segregation — in the 21st century this may mean establishing virtual organisations with porous boundaries;
- occasional failure is more powerful than constant success. This is because calculated risks create learning.

In combination, then, optimising, catalysing and leveraging become an immensely powerful combination.

If you're a funder, planner or coordinating agency, you will probably leverage best by:

- building network capacity, and not that which is directly funded or planned

- recognising the scope of the entire portfolio to which you belong — and in doing so reducing duplication
- creating shared understandings and common value assumptions (see Chapter 1 in Part 2, 'Common Goals create Common Good')
- partnering with complementary institutions and businesses
- creating structures for self-generative ideas — being less prescriptive
- offering incentives for sharing ideas with high return on investment
- provide arms-length funding to agencies with a greater capacity for risk

If you're a program or service deliverer, your strategy will involve optimising:

- coordination — reduce gaps and coordination failures
- evidence — do what works
- capability — build competencies that predict performance
- continuous improvement — fix broken parts of your system

So where are breakthrough returns on investment to be found? Remember that single solutions only fix the problems they were designed to solve. To solve exponentially increasing problems, the most intelligent use of dollars is in partnership approaches which *leverage agencies who have already optimised.*

Key mindset question: Do you really need more money, or do you need to find ways to spend the money you have differently?

- Who are your partners in creating shared value?

- How can you get your staff and clients/customers to help you optimise?

- Are your leaders able to identify the major levers in your sector by which investment can be multiplied?

- Do leaders at the most senior level fully understand linear, optimised and leveraged growth?

6

Shifting power to your clients

'Institutions will try to preserve the problem for which they are the solution.'

CLAY SHIRKY

Open the newspapers in any major city across the Western world and you're likely to see calls for more teachers, more police, more nurses and more doctors. And who's usually asking? It's often the public, who want to feel better protected, educated and treated. Or tellingly, it's the professions themselves, or their unions. But should we listen to them? Are they in fact the best authorities?

The dirty word here is power. This is masked behind labels like 'client-centred', 'patient-led' and 'self-determined'.

After all, these were the stated rationales for the large-scale de-institutionalisation of the (admittedly dismal) psychiatric and disability facilities in the USA (and to a lesser extent countries like Australia and the UK) from the 1980s on. Those who were de-institutionalised didn't, on the whole, get self-determination or any semblance of patient-led care. Instead they got one of two things. Either 'look after yourself' — you can walk the streets of any large American city to see what I mean — or for a lucky few, a replacement form of congregate care. This mostly meant group homes and activity centres that provided better quality of support, but still within a paradigm of passive care.

Anyone to the Left of Ayn Rand can readily see what's wrong with 'look after yourself' for vulnerable people with complex needs, but what's wrong with the passive care model?

The answer is simple:

- across every form of in-person support (medical, psychological, disability, and aged care) costs are sky-rocketing
- they require vast armies of expensive professionals
- they create extra dependencies which further increase costs
- multiple needs create coordination costs

I'm not espousing Clay Shirky's position — that police encourage crime to keep themselves in a job, or doctors and hospitals collude to keep the sick unwell. But health professionals often fail to fully utilise the single most valuable medical tool in their dispensary: the patient.

It's a cliché to say that no-one can motivate you except yourself, yet we design, fund and deliver a multitude of services founded on expert-led diagnoses and interventions (not just in health, but in everything from education to financial services). This creates a user-dependence where well-meaning providers direct and advise the user without also facilitating their independence. Satisfaction increases for a time but at a certain point, the outcomes of the intervention start to drop off. This is because responsibility for their maintenance sits with the professional, and fails to fully embrace the imperative of their client's own motivation and volition. If you doubt this, ask yourself if you've ever had a financial professional prepare a savings or investment plan for you, or a doctor recommend a diet or exercise plan. How well did they do in keeping you to it?

However, there is an irony in all this self-management in today's world. On the one hand, we do far *less for ourselves than we used to*. Think of the number of meals you eat out; about who cleans your house or car. It's rare nowadays for us to build our own furniture or sew our own clothing. These are, after all, mostly products or services that are highly commodified — and easily replaceable. On the other hand, we can if we wish, do a lot *more for ourselves that used to be the sole domain of a professional class*. I don't need a publisher to author a book such as this, for example, or a webmaster to design my website. I don't need a photo processor or print company to reproduce my photos or artwork. In these instances, I self-manage my own self-established goals. What I say to my clients, therefore, is this:

1. if your clients need commodified services that are *cheap and convenient* (for them, not you) do it for them (or find someone else to)
2. if their outcome is a self-established goal, and the support they need is *expensive or inconvenient*, find new ways of transferring maximum expertise to them.

We'll spend our remaining time in this chapter looking at the second of these.

People with chronic health conditions (like heart disease, arthritis or asthma) often experience a seriously compromised quality of life. Their mobility is affected and they're often in pain, which of course impacts upon their social and economic lives. Poor management of their condition may even mean their premature death. In the lower left of the diagram opposite, you can see how for these people simply doing nothing — letting

Four levels of self-directedness and the pathways between them

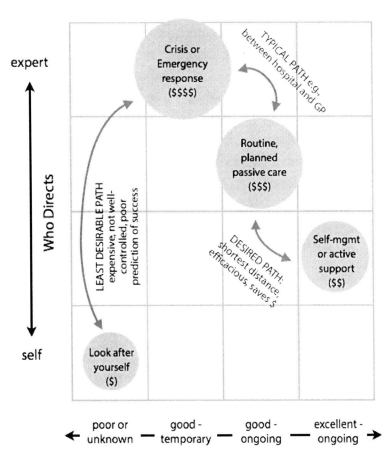

them 'look after themselves', means that costs are low certainly (the size of the bubbles indicates expenditure per person), but so are the outcomes.

Another approach is to simply do nothing, and use the emergency departments as your primary treatment option. Here, temporarily at least, effectiveness is good, but cost is prohibitively high. That leaves two remaining possibilities. First, the conventional routine care, in the hands of the health professional. Almost certainly, this will yield good, and ongoing results, although the cost still remains moderately high. Our goal is a solution that will reduce costs *and* turn good results into excellent ones.

That magic bullet is often (though not always) increased self-management. By this we mean both DIY (do-it-yourself) *and* KIY (know-it-yourself). For people with chronic conditions who self-manage, we know two things. First, they mostly get better outcomes. That is, they learn how to deal with pain and frustration themselves; and they can self-improve their strength, flexibility and endurance. They learn how to use and regulate their medications, they can communicate with family and professionals about their condition, they know what to eat (and what not to) and they know how to evaluate new treatments proposed by their doctors. Second, about eighty per cent of the self-management skills listed above *are the same, whether you've got heart disease, diabetes, arthritis or even schizophrenia.*

In another context (like disability, aged care, homelessness, problem gambling or crime prevention) self-management will *look* very different but the same basic principle applies. That is, *behavioural change is not dependent on a condition and its manifestations* (pain, poverty level, etcetera); *it is dependent on a person's feelings of self-efficacy* (a belief that one is capable of performing in a way to reach a set of goals). The power of this is that self-efficacy reinforces itself. I believe more in my ability to control my symptoms as I notice my symptoms being controlled!

Here are four practical design features that will create the optimal conditions for people to *regulate themselves*:

- **The best guides are the ones who've been there**. Programs led by professionals get no better outcomes and are usually considerably more expensive than those taught by peer instructors. And they don't always have to be real: virtual social networking shows the same gains as in-person networking for some conditions.
- **Sharply reduce mixed messages**. Over fifty per cent of people with a serious chronic condition receive more than one diagnosis for the same problem within a one-year period. Creating single portals for diagnosis and delivery of

advice will ameliorate this.

- **Move from knowing to doing, fast**. Create action plans/ contracts with durability and follow-up. Offer mechanisms for self-diagnosis and monitoring with unambiguous triggers points for action (personal health informatics like glucose monitors, for example). Build in successive approximations, feedback and support for process improvements.

- **It's not enough to work with the person, you must work within their contexts**. The best success in self-management comes from being around exemplars of success. It's harder for overweight people to lose weight surrounded by obese friends for example, or for prisoners to go straight while they're in gaol. Surround people with messages that reinforce positive actions. As far as you can, make sure the goals of communities are linked to the goals of health/social service systems — with connections to prevention/lifestyle modification.

We started this chapter with a comment about power. Won't experts, practitioners and professionals feel *disempowered* as they transfer power to their clients, patients and service-users? Of course they will, if they continue to see themselves as guardians of secret knowledge or wavers of magic wands. Won't they be rightfully cautious that self-managing patients will absorb a bunch of semi-fictitious urban myths and convince themselves somehow that they're the peer of the specialist? Yes, this can happen too. However, if professionals slowly change their conception of what the ideal role of an expert is, neither scenario is likely. The new role becomes one of builders of systems that *purposely abrogate primary personal responsibility to our users/ clients*. If anything, within such a mindshift, the expert has a more important job than ever, with tasks such as:

- **diagnosis** — reducing the noise and ambiguity of conflicting signals that tell the patient what's really happening
- **evidence accumulation** — establishing best/alternative courses of action
- **message creation** — translating complex and ambivalent material into actionable forms
- **navigation** — supporting a person who's confused by the system to find their optimal path
- **resource targeting** — helping patients get the services and supports they need
- **coordination** — getting various activities lined up in a way that makes sense — and gets good results.

In this model, perhaps the main challenge for experts is to understand that for self-efficacy to grow, *the condition is not the main game*. It's not about managing a specific condition, it's about managing the effects of the comorbidities, or conditions that go along with it, such as depression and anxiety. The greatest value in self-management therefore, is to constructively manage emotional responses to the condition — so one of the most powerful things you can do is to build systems that provide assistance in mindfulness and emotional state management.

Key mindset question: How can what you offer remain viable unless you increase the ability of your clients/patients to self-manage?

- What self-management paradigm are you pursuing?

- How do your experts see their roles?

- Can you create systems that increase the generic self-management skills of your patients/clients?

PART 2

ACT DIFFERENTLY

The 21st century's most influential people will be integrators. Integrators get multiple partners with different interests to shift their thinking, in unison. I call these 'convergent contributions'. To get convergent contributions, we need people who are masterful in six areas:

- Building common goals create common good
- Harnessing group insight for positive action
- Capturing people's motivation for change
- Focussing on the fixable
- Finding connections among contributors
- Encouraging interdependency and symbiotic effort

1

ACT DIFFERENTLY

Creating common goals for common good

'In the white water rapids, each ant thinks it's in charge of the log.'

DON BECK

It's a truism that in times of conflict we need to spend time and effort working on common goals. But how should groups, often of diverse and disparate interests, motivations and constituencies do this? Take two examples. First, a dispossessed Palestinian whose family home was taken by Israeli settlers in the 1940s. How would you set a common goal here? Second, a more commonplace example — a sporting team in a cut-throat competition. Let's say it's a surf life saving club and its members are from all walks of life, with 'diamond-in-the-rough' truck

Getting to common goals requires a question and a conversation

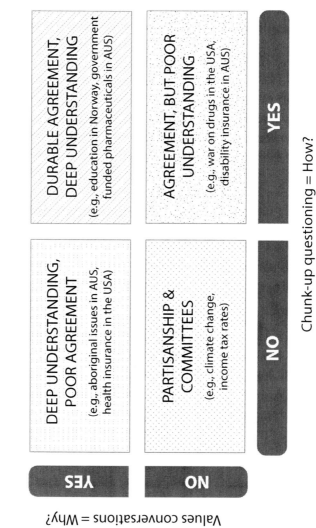

Values conversations = Why?

	NO	YES
YES	DEEP UNDERSTANDING, POOR AGREEMENT (e.g., aboriginal issues in AUS, health insurance in the USA)	DURABLE AGREEMENT, DEEP UNDERSTANDING (e.g., education in Norway, government funded pharmaceuticals in AUS)
NO	PARTISANSHIP & COMMITTEES (e.g., climate change, income tax rates)	AGREEMENT, BUT POOR UNDERSTANDING (e.g., war on drugs in the USA, disability insurance in AUS)

Chunk-up questioning = How?

drivers rubbing shoulders with top-end-of-town lawyers.

In both instances, there are three basic tools that enable very high quality common goals to be formed. Two are dialogue techniques, and one's a simple sleight-of-mouth that can defuse any discussion, no matter how heated. The first of these is 'chunking up', in other words, looking for a generalised understanding — for overall purpose and meaning.

Typical questions to help chunk up are:

- why are we doing this?
- how will we know when we're really successful?
- if we had X, what would it enable us to get?
- what's the single most important thing for us right now?
- what does X mean for us?

This technique was used to brilliant effect by Don Beck, the social theorist and activist who worked with Palestinian villagers in efforts to reach agreement with Israeli authorities regarding the redistribution of land. Not unexpectedly, many villages were resistant to the Israeli agenda and tensions were running high. One Palestinian villager angrily shouted, 'I still have the key to my grandfather's house! Honour demands that I get it back!'

With thoughtful questioning and a conciliatory approach, Beck eventually established that what was more important than the house, or even honour, was being a 'real man'. He won agreement by saying, 'You want to be a real man? Then *build* something that will make your children and grandchildren proud of you!' They listened, nodded, and agreed.

This technique will ensure agreement on a goal, but not necessarily guarantee a genuine understanding of *why* the goal is desirable. Successful people will implicitly understand this next type of conversation because they have them often, without understanding their underlying structure. My wife's stepfather Bob has had three successful careers (government, accounting and the law). This doesn't include sport, in which he was an all-rounder; an accomplished footballer, cyclist, and surf life saver. In the last of these, he coached a team of outside runners to become national champions and would describe how he'd 'install' different motivations for team members, with clarion calls such as:

- 'If we don't get through this round, we're finished'
- 'If we stick together, we can achieve anything'
- 'Train your butt off or be kicked out; we're A-team players only here'
- 'We will win because we know the rules better than anyone else'
- 'This is a pivotal time in your life – success here sets you up

to achieve anything in life'
- 'Everyone has a vital part to play; back each other up'.

Each of these statements triggers one of six fundamentally different systems of values. Read the above list again and you'll see they are appeals to deep-seated drives in us all for survival, tribalism, power, compliance, opportunity and equality. Bob knew that each team member possessed a different constellation of these values, even if they have the same common goal. Bob knew that each team member possessed a different constellation of values, even if they have the same common goal. His job as coach was therefore to provide 'tilts and nudges', sparking those that are 'active systems' to maximise their motivational impact.

Magicians use sleight-of-hand to redirect the audiences attention away from something they don't want you to see and towards what they do want you to see. In this way, you can use a sleight-of-mouth to redirect people towards agreement. The easiest way, for example, to negate someone's opinion is to start your reply with the word 'but'. As soon as you do that, it implies that you're about to oppose them. Therefore, the icing on the cake of common goal formation is to replace 'but' with 'and'.

To do this, *chunk up* to a point where you can find merit in the other person's viewpoint. For example, in a heated discussion where your counterpart is arguing that pharmacists oughtn't be allowed to prescribe drugs, you might respond with, 'I agree that we need to keep prescribing and dispensing separate, as it could be abused. And, I do believe that pharmacists can take much more responsibility than they do within our health system'. This at least keeps the discussion moving and you can start to explore how pharmacists can expand their contribution.

Whether you're a leader, a facilitator or a negotiator, chunking up, triggering values systems and using 'and, not but' will dramatically transform the quality of understanding between diverse parties, as well as the durability of the agreements they reach.

Key actions towards the creation of shared goals

1. Invite people to complete 'chunk up' phrases such as:
- 'we exist so that…'
- 'we know we are successful when…'
- the single most important thing for us now is…'

2. Use alignment questions to elicit values systems:
- 'what keeps us all together is...' (tribalism)
- 'what would make us look good is…' (power)
- 'what we are mandated to do is…' (compliance)
- 'what would create tremendous opportunity for us is…' (opportunity)
- 'what our constituents ask us to do is…' (equality)

3. Use 'and not but' in contentious conversations, either one-to-one or in groups, whether as participant or facilitator. It will work.

2 ACT DIFFERENTLY

Harnessing group insight for positive action

'I have often seen people climbing the ladder of success only to find it is put against the wrong wall.'

JOSEPH CAMPBELL

There's a prevailing myth which is that if we innovate, we will find solutions to our problems. This is reflected in the fact that if you search Google for the term 'innovation' you'll get half a *billion* results (and counting). Even a search for 'public sector innovation' turns up 35 million pages. What does this tell us? That we are obsessed with innovation, and possibly because we have two oversimplified and misguided views about innovation as the solution to all problems. The first is based on the myth of the uniquely creative hero (think Steve Jobs or

Thomas Edison) who possesses personal attributes of tenacity and vision in pursuit of a world-changing objective. The second is its opposite, that innovation can be learned by anyone and applied anywhere. This has become a mini-industry — Amazon lists almost 50,000 books on the subject.

In fact, there are problems with innovation in most organisations, including that:

- it's in the hands of the creative class only, who come up with excellent but ultimately unrealistic solutions;
- it's put into the hands of risk managers or, even worse, lawyers, who eliminate anything creative; and/or
- it's poorly understood and therefore unsupported by the executive suite, who are more focused on short-term accountability and compliance to the wishes of shareholders, public or elected representatives.

I prefer to say that we don't need more innovation per se. What we need are *groups that can develop insights which are actionable*. First, let's ask who has been exceptional at this? I'd argue two candidates: the creativity and business acumen of Walt Disney over his entire working lifetime, and the pharmaceutical industry's ability to bring highly effective drugs to market. While neither of these examples are without failures — and even controversies — they are certainly not one-trick ponies;

they each have delivered their 'innovations' over and over again.

What exactly did they do, and how?

Disney's achievement was to create an unparalleled string of commercially *and* creatively successful animated movies, starting with Mickey Mouse in the 1930s and continuing with regular hits until his death in 1966. To this day, Disney (as an individual) has the most Academy Awards ever (22 awards from 59 nominations) and Disney is still the largest player in the global entertainment industry almost fifty years after his death. In the Golden Age of animation of the 1930s and 1940s, he was a notable figure not just creatively but technically — Disney himself invented a type of camera that allowed cartoons a sense of depth and also introduced stereo sound to movies.

Over his lifetime, Disney produced some 680 films (mostly short animations) and 19 full-length animated features, nearly all of which remain household names. Think Snow White and Seven Dwarfs, Bambi, Fantasia, The Jungle Book….it's a long list. The vast majority were creative *and* commercial successes. This is no coincidence. Disney organised his work so it *guaranteed* creative, innovative outcomes. His revolutionary approach[1] kept his staff

---

[1] The first person to describe Disney's innovation strategy in detail was Robert Dilts. See Dilts (1994) Strategies of Genius: Volume 1 - Aristotle, Sherlock Holmes, Walt Disney, Wolfgang Amadeus Mozart, Meta Publications and Dilts (1991) Tools for dreamers : strategies for creativity

focused in their thinking and design of a particular project. It involved three rooms:

- **The Dreamers' Lounge**: This was a comfortable room where ideas were spun, dreams were harvested, no concept was too crazy, and ridiculous hunches and inspirations were laughed at but also then developed to their logical (or illogical) extremes.
- **The Realists' Workshop**: The 'dreams' from the first room were coordinated and story-boards created (which was another Disney innovation) that placed characters and events into a sequence. Some worked, but the majority bombed.
- **The Critics' Cupboard**: At first, this was literally a small room under a staircase, where the whole crew would offer a no-holds-barred critique of works emanating from the Realist Room. It was always the work that was criticised, never the individual.

If a work survived the Critics' Cupboard, it was ready for production; if it didn't, it went back to the Dreamer's Room for further work. The key, Disney found, was to allow each of these processes to occur in their own time and space and, sometimes, with their own people who specialised in each form of thinking.

---

and the structure of innovation. Meta Publications.

This is not at all dissimilar in structure to the process that pharmaceutical drugs go through, on their way from discovery to the pharmacy shelf. Nearly everyone reading these words will have pharmaceutical drugs to thank for being here: our lifespans have risen dramatically in the past seventy years and pharmaceutical drugs are a major contributor (along with public health measures and general improvements in prosperity). For the eight year lifespan gain of the last twenty years, about two-thirds is attributable to newer and better drugs to treat and prevent illness. Even improvements in labour productivity have been shown to be in small part (about one per cent annually) the result of drugs that reduce absenteeism from chronic illnesses[2]. This is a significant achievement with significant costs, mostly borne by what is known as 'Big Pharma' — the top twenty pharmaceutical companies that each spend more than five hundred million annually on research and development (R&D). For example, global R&D in 2010 was roughly sixty billion dollars (against global revenues of $600 billion). A single new drug will cost in the region of two billion dollars to bring it to market and between discovery and full regulatory approval ten years may elapse.

These companies are naturally nothing like Disney and each pursue a dramatically different approach to their R&D activities,

___

[2] See http://www.washingtonpost.com/wp-dyn/content/article/2007/07 /10/AR2007071001468.html

but there are parallels — if we recognise that all pharmaceutical drugs pass through three types of proofs:

1. proof of **mechanism**: this is the earliest stage of drug development (before it's ever given to humans or animals) and aims to show that the drug's components interact biochemically in the desired way.
2. proof of **concept**: this is when the drug is trialled on humans, aiming to establish if the desired levels of clinical activity exist, how the drug is absorbed, distributed, metabolised and excreted, and what the right doses should be, based on tolerance and interactions with other drugs.
3. proof of **principle**: this is like Disney's cupboard, the litmus test, where much larger groups of patients use the drug, in different durations, and in randomised comparison with other drugs, as well as placebos. This proof aims to give an assessment of efficacy and safety in real world conditions.

Put Walt Disney and Big Pharma together and what do you get? A way of structuring discussions — and an iterative process for innovation — that can be undertaken by groups, especially disparate groups. The diagram opposite shows how it works. The dreamers' job is to come up with a proof of mechanism:

*   what's the result or outcome we're all seeking?
*   what possible methods/interventions/activities might get us there?

- who could participate/lead/fund?
- what are *all* the resources available? How could these be combined, or used more flexibly?

The realists' task is to arrive at a proof of concept:

- is there any evidence that the proposed actions will lead to the desired outcome?
- are these within tolerances (human, financial, organisational, reputational, political)?
- who should participate and to what degree. This is akin to asking 'what's the marketable dose?' in pharmaceutical development.

The critics' function is to help create proof-of-principle via actual testing:

- what variations occurred or could occur? Are these acceptable?
- are our early results scalable? How big could we make this?
- is it safe?

You can easily see that if you ask the critic questions ('Is this safe?') too early, it will stymie the creative, early-stage dreamer conversation. Equally, if you let dreamers infect critics — once trials have occurred — with questions like, 'What if we did it this way?' it will defocus and possibly derail the project.

Generating actionable insights in groups

Is the result worthwhile?
Are the interactions sound?
Can people and materials
be found?

Dreamer
*Proof of
Mechanism*

Realist
Proof of Concept

Is likely variation
acceptable?
How scalable is
this?
Is it safe?

Will the desired
actions occur?
Are they within our
tolerances?
What's the right level
of intervention?

Critic
Proof of Principle

All of these functions are critical and each has its place. If you cultivate these — in both leaders and teams, internally and in partnership — you will almost certainly create groups who can innovate at will or, more accurately, develop insights that are actionable, just like Walt Disney, and the most successful pharmaceutical companies.

Key actions to create actionable insights

In the dreamer (proof of mechanism) phase, four powerful ways to 'dream' are to:

- capture **client insights** — what reframes/ improvements can our clients offer us?
- **horizon scan** — what other problems will success here require us to solve?
- harvest **expertise** — what do others know that will be helpful?
- **drag-'n'-drop** — what can we learn from other dissimilar areas?

In the realist (proof of concept) phase, three of the most powerful question domains are (in this order):

- **opportunity** — if we spend time on X, what does it mean we could do more of/better? On the other hand, what does it mean we can't do?
- **evidence** — is there a body of best-practice and if so, what does it tell us? If there isn't, is this a chance to create one?

- **accountability** — what are the key tasks and who will own them?

In the critic (proof of principle) phase, four solid risk-mitigation question domains are:

- **failure** — what if X doesn't work and we lose our investment?
- **efficiency** — could X prolong our existing processes or introduces discontinuities?
- **process/regulatory** — in trying X, what if we can't obtain approvals, permissions, or support?
- **reputational** — if X isn't a resounding success, will partners, funders and clients see us as weak or ineffective?

111

3 ACT DIFFERENTLY

Capturing people's motivation for change

'The real art of conducting consists in transitions.'
GUSTAV MAHLER

We are living in a world where constant, simultaneous large-scale change is the new normal. Probably much like your own, the organisations I work with are very commonly involved in change that is:

- constant (before one cycle is finished, another one's started)
- simultaneous (several change programs are operating at the same time)
- large-scale (they affect large numbers of people in major ways)

Change leaders usually struggle with three things:

1. Moving from your current results to your desired results is not linear, and it's not fully controllable;
2. It's difficult getting the change idea from the heads of a few visionaries into the hearts and minds of many; and
3. It can be arduous — and costly — to create an implementable reality from an initial vague intention or imperative.

They key to creating change-readiness across an organisation (or a partnership) is understanding that change is *not a top-down linear process*. It's a *dialectic*: two things have to happen at the same time, which interact and sometimes contradict each other. That is, that we want to make an abstract idea more and more concrete (this is called instantiation) and at *the same time*, we need to get more people to understand it at a deep level (this is called translation).

And, there's another layer to add to the dialectic complexity. Change is iterative: you want to create more and more focused cycles of thinking and doing, and testing both reactions and consequences. This means that successfully building change-readiness nearly always passes through the following four thresholds over time (illustrated as the four grey bubbles opposite):

Increasing change readiness requires two forces acting together

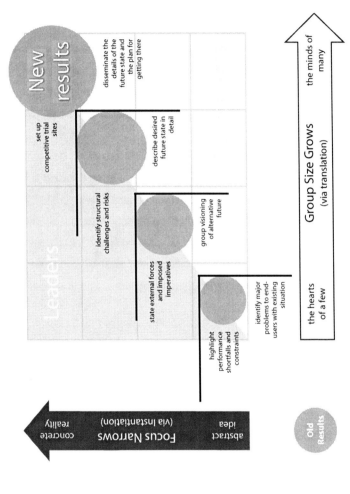

1. the *prospect* for change is seen as acceptable, that is, there's a belief that the organisation should change.
2. the *specific improvement* is agreed to be sensible — there's a belief in the destination.
3. the *methods* are approved of as reasonable — there's belief in the impact of the interventions.
4. the *plan* is deemed achievable if everyone participates — people believe in the value of their role in the plan.

I've watched leaders sometimes do this in reverse — and all at once. Think about whether you've heard these sorts of podium speeches from senior executives:

'We need everyone to be on board with this. The plan is {insert endless powerpoint slides}. The methods we've chosen are {insert initiatives drawn from the executive table or from an expensive consulting firm}. These will ensure X and improve Y. Please don't be mistaken; we're not doing this for {insert the greatest fears of employees e.g., cost-cutting}. Ultimately we're doing this so that {insert motherhood statements}. I hope we can rely on everyone's support and full cooperation'.

And that's exactly what they'll do: *hope*. The problem with this approach is that these leaders are starting from the rather old-fashioned and authoritarian premise that:

1. If an idea's sound, people will accept it
2. If enough people accept it, they will change
3. If enough people change, the desired results will occur

The method I'll share with you addresses two critical problems. In instantiation (moving from the abstract idea to a real plan) too many good ideas are simply left on the table because not enough people get involved. What if these ideas are worth a lot of money (either in outcomes or revenues/savings), or they happen to be the critical success factors? Second, in translation, a core characteristic of many change projects is an appreciable number of people who resist/sabotage change. What if the saboteurs have the power to stop the change in its tracks? Or if they do such a good job that it not only prevents *this* change, but other changes as well?

In the diagram, you can see that successful change is very simply defined: it's moving from current results to desired future results. The mechanisms are simple too: instantiation, or turning an abstract idea into a concrete reality (the vertical axis) and translation — with a few mobilising the next critical mass, who then mobilise their network of influence, and so on (the horizontal axis).

You can also see that the grid is split diagonally in two, as change requires both leaders and followers (or participants). Together, these equal the total number of change-ready participants. Your job is to maximise this number. In the upper left (darker grey) triangle, there are things that *only* leaders can do. In the lower right (white triangle) there are things in which followers *must* be involved. The reason these are separated is that often, leaders and professional 'change managers' take responsibility for *all* of these.

LEADERS' RESPONSIBILITIES (with decreasing involvement over time)

1. To quantify performance shortfalls or resource constraints, and their implications into the future.
2. To powerfully and accurately reflect the imperatives on the organisation, both external (those imposed by the operating environment, funders, the regulator framework, policy imperatives and the like) or internal (board policy or shareholder/owner demands).
3. To identify structural challenges and risks - both strategic and operational.
4. To establish trial sites (preferably competitive) with learning cycles

FOLLOWERS' RESPONSIBILITIES (with participation broadening over time)

1. To identify and quantify problems to end-users/customers/clients/patients from the current system
2. To foster a shared view of an ideal future
3. To help design the specifics of that future state in detail
4. To promote the future state and the plan for getting there

They key to doing the above well lies in understanding the interlocking nature of the leaders' and followers' tasks. When we look at this way by combining them, we see the following:

Leaders' *and* **Followers' STEP 1 is genuine problem-sharing**

Any true transformation starts with a deep understanding of the severity of a complex problem. Pressure for change is explicitly stated in terms of:

i. the problems of end-users, that is, they're suffering, they're not getting the results they deserve, they're inconvenienced and confused by an adversarial system; and
ii. resource constraints, such as growth in service demand, funding constraints, unreliable or absent public support, or workforce availability.

The first part of this — problems to end-users — speaks to achieving buy-in. The closer to the mark you are with this, they more visceral, 'a-ha' responses you'll get. The second part of this, problem-sharing around resource constraints, is also the first stage in concretising. It helps you work out what some of the drivers of the solution are likely to be.

Leaders' *and* **Followers' STEP 2 is authorising change**

Address the two dimensions above simultaneously by blending external mandates or imperatives with group visioning. The result should be a set of change principles (not specific outcomes) from the top. Examples in this regard include 'the conversion of passive welfare recipients into contributing taxpayers', 'heighten social inclusion of marginalised and disadvantaged', 'shorter, less costly interventions', or 'clients considered as whole people, not a set of specific needs'.

In other words, what should exist is a clear and shared sense that the focus is on the *right improvement*. The authorising stage is also when the change team is nominated. Preferably, this is not just any team, but one with three essential ingredients: intellectual firepower; organisational credibility; and project management clout. The job of this team will be to create a working concept in a brief (though realistic) timeframe, say ninety days, or six months.

Leaders' *and* **Followers' STEP 3 is creating future possibilities**

On the translational dimension, use the collective wisdom of leaders, followers, participants, experts, clients and customers to create a clear systems model of the desired change: 'What does it look, feel and sound like?' As part of this process, you will need to capture all major conceptual distinctions. Use diagrams, statements of desirable experience, labels and key words. Create sub-systems (for service delivery, for decision-making) that can be built from existing ingredients (ours or others). Convey how change is *different* from the status quo.

On the instantiation dimension, identify immediate structural challenges. How can we identify best practice? How will we get political support? How do we intend to work with legacy systems, and create workforce transformation? What are our defining terms and what models do we need to develop? What communications will best mobilise buy-in? Cast these as 'ninety-day challenges' or 'six-month must-do's' otherwise they'll lurk forever as ammunition for skeptics.

Leaders' *and* **Followers' STEP 4 is doing by showing**

To fine-tune the instantiation, develop criteria for trial sites/ test bases and carry out competitive recruitment to heighten desirability. Get real people doing real work and helping to develop the new paradigms required. Make sure that they create learning loops of generalisable experience and build tools that others can use.

Simultaneously, disseminate your project more and more broadly. Publicise early successes from the trial/test sites. Create a timescale for the various practical shifts you'll want to make (A then B, then C, through to Z if necessary). Circulate leaders from trial sites to 'show how it's done' to others. Always focus on outcomes and make as much learning as possible peer-to-peer. Respond meaningfully to any culturally-based concerns that the new ways present.

When you do this, on large and smaller-scale change projects, you'll notice that you'll harness some elemental truths about how people operate in groups:

- groups — and entire institutions — have volition
- people have a natural impulse for improvement
- people naturally seek out leaders
- people want to participate in something worthy
- people have a strong desire to understand something new

Organisations that adopt these steps end up achieving what the desire. They grasp that:

- *more* change isn't necessarily better, but executing a handful of the most critical changes most definitely is

- change can't be managed or controlled, but is generated *organically*
- a good idea is enough to start with, *but that's all it is*
- people can't be compelled to change, only *invited* to join you on the change journey

Key actions in creating change readiness

Identify those among your leaders who can instantiate. Not everyone can do this. The main mindset needed is an ability to think backwards from outcomes and not just the other way around (See Part 1, Chapter 4, Measure What Matters the Most).

Select the groups who will form the critical mass at each stage of translation. You'll want successively larger groups, but begin with those who are both capable of thinking strategically and are of influence within the organisation. Don't worry about hierarchy or position, pick people who can think well and represent the ideas effectively to others in their circle.

To deal with skepticism, work at *the previous level* to that which the skepticism occurs. If participation is low, consider whether the right trials and tests have been selected and if appropriate dissemination and translation has occurred. If the methodology is being criticised, ask yourself whether the structural factors/risks are well considered and if your future vision is adequately described.

4 ACT DIFFERENTLY

Focusing on the fixable

'Those who know how to think need no teachers.'
MAHATMA GANDHI

I have lost count of the number of times I've read the throwaway phrase 'address needs' — as in 'We aim to comprehensively address all the needs of our clients' or 'Community needs will be addressed within the strategic plan'.

But how do we work out *which* needs can be realistically addressed?

Imagine the quintessential Australian town of Desertville. It's remote, with vast agricultural fields on one side; and on the other sandy scrub that extends for thousands of kilometres. Its 50,000 locals are proud of the town they've carved out in this hostile landscape. They're down-to-earth, no-nonsense people. But they have a problem. Violent crime is creeping upwards. Last year, it went up by more than ten per cent. People are increasingly fearful to go out at night. Sometimes there are fights on the streets, and children are scared to ride their bikes to school. It's been headline news in the local paper for months.

Some people point what they believe is the obvious rationale — 'It's the grog' or 'it's out-of-town blow-ins causing trouble'. Others argue, 'If you look at the hard facts, it's mainly young men. Eighty-five per cent of crime is committed by under-25s'. Others still might say, 'The causes are too numerous and too complex to deal with. What we need are more police with stronger powers'. Their opponents counter with, 'The causes are obvious: it's about unemployment and disadvantage. That's what we've got to fix'. Finally, the bureaucrats and management echelons will say, 'We're hamstrung in terms of resources; we're not getting any more dollars'.

There are two standard solutions in such cases: *do nothing*, or *do everything*. The first of these is pretty obvious and the most common. The second of these is a little like the wedding banquet planner who aims to please everyone by offering pasta, seafood, salads, kebabs, pizzas, fried chicken and ten different desserts. It's all there, but nothing is done well. In Desertville's case, this would mean police patrolling the Indigenous camps on

Desertville's outskirts more often, offering self-defence training for young people, equipping women with anti-assault sprays, restricting the sale of alcohol, and installing closed-circuit cameras outside nightclubs.

Is there an *addressable* need here? And how to disentangle it from the mush of statistics, opinion and hobby-horses?

Rather than ask, 'What can we do about this?' a far more useful question is, 'How do we work out what needs are *addressable*?' Our starting point has to be that any single determinant of what's addressable will not pass muster. Data alone (the top left quadrant) isn't enough. What people *think* is important (upper right) won't cut it. It's sometimes tempting to go with whatever people will agree to (lower right), but that too is faulty. And, finally, I've lost count of the number of times people have accepted a solution simply because someone's offered to fund it (lower left). All of these, singly, are usually doomed to fail.

Instead, they have to be taken together, but in a very definite sequence, and possibly even with different participants, as illustrated by the arrows in the diagram. We must convert evidence to meaningful facts, and use these to engage a community and gain agreement. We need to convert resolutions into project plans; manage the resultant action; and measure the results. Taken together, these actions will highlight and justify

Working out what needs are addressable

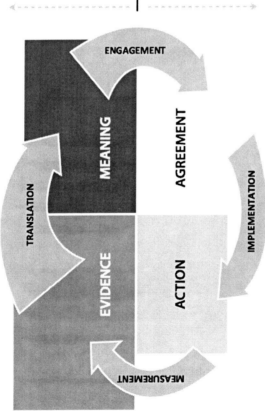

ENGAGEMENT

MEANING

AGREEMENT

TRANSLATION

EVIDENCE

ACTION

IMPLEMENTATION

MEASUREMENT

Leadership =
ensuring relevance

Management =
ensuring effectiveness

Left brain = logical, objective | Right Brain = intuitive, subjective

the smallest number of highest-impact interventions, with the support of both the informed professionals and the populace. In the case of Desertville, the partners who came together were the city government, police, justice department, children and family services, the public housing agency, welfare agencies, schools and Aboriginal groups.

1. Evidence: What does the data tell us is happening?

The police data presented a startling irony: Desertville police were amongst the most successful in the state at solving crimes. However, rates of crime kept increasing. Senior police concluded that 'locking people up just doesn't work'. The local data also showed two interesting things. For such a small town, there were a lot of young people who were repeat offenders for public offences – in the streets, parks, bars, and car parks. Police spent a significant portion of their time attending and processing such cases. But this wasn't the majority of police work. The data clearly showed that close to half of all police call-outs were in response to private assaults, or family/domestic violence.

2. Meaning: What does this mean for people like us?

It's important that the next stage is interpretative, that is, it asks, 'Now that we know this, what's important to people like us?' In the case of Desertville, it was well known that in the case of both public and private (domestic) violence the town was dealing with relatively small numbers of persistent reoffenders.

Furthermore, the agencies involved mostly knew exactly who those reoffenders were. They're the ones picked up by police, the ones (or their kids) reported as non-attending by schools, assisted by welfare agencies, and housed by public housing agencies. 'What's important to us', this group said, 'is that those who reoffended are somehow helped *not* to'.

3. Agreement: How could this situation change?

The next question is one about engagement, and discovering 'What makes people tick?' We know that these reoffenders are mostly poorly-educated, volatile young men. They don't listen to authority figures, let alone social workers, doctors or teachers. In fact, they pride themselves on resisting them. So in this case, to answer 'what makes people tick' lay in considering the people to which reoffenders *do* actually listen. In Desertville, this group's influencers were found in their families (a father, cousin, or brother) and among their peers.

4. Action: What can be observed, measured and managed?

The planning group decided that in a community as small as Desertville, it would be feasible to find the six top 'frequent flyers' — those who reoffended the *most*. The plan was to find influential people in their families/social groups and then direct high-level intensive resources (coaching, health-care, job assistance, psychological services) *at them*, aimed at keeping the frequent flyer out of trouble. For each person, the approach would be tailored to their particular circumstances. Even if this cost $50,000 per person, it would be a good investment, given that these frequent flyers used up a disproportionate amount of local resources, and they were 'on the books' of every enforcement and support agency in town. The measures of success were agreed and included factors such as number of police callouts, attendance at school by family members, reduced injury levels and hospital admissions. Finally, there was tightly controlled feedback about which was reported back to the six individuals' families.

Displaying this as quadrants also helps us recognise two further features. The upper quadrants are largely the domain of leaders. Their job is to determine what's relevant, sort the valuable wheat from the useless chaff, the be heard above the din of vested and opinionated other parties. The lower quadrants are management functions — the ability to turn agreements into implementable actions, deliver on these, and report and evaluate. It's not just valuable, but *vital* to recognise these differences and put the right people on each job.

Second, the left and the right of the diagram almost reflect the concept of 'left brain — right brain'. On the left — from implementation to action and onto measurement — best results will be achieved by those who are logical, objective and rational. The right hand side translates data into meaningful messages, and gains the trust and commitment of others. This requires an altogether different set of 'right brain' qualities — a strong intuitive grasp of subjective and, often, emotive issues.

The skills needed, therefore, for each quadrant are quite different and as follows:

1. Evidence to Meaning (LB): analysis and translation
2. Meaning to Agreement (RB): communications and engagement
3. Agreement to Action (LB): facilitation and co-design
4. Action to Research (RB): project management and evaluation

This suggests clearly that a single person or even a single organisation cannot work out what need is actually addressable but, rather, relies on a partnership approach in which many people combine their unique expertise and outlooks.

Determining which needs can be addressed and which cannot

Start with data. Make sure the data addresses the right questions. If during the engagement phase new and different questions arise, go back to the data.

Put the right people on the right tasks. Don't make working out addressable needs the job of one person, one team, or even one organisation. Map out whom in your community will be ideally suited to lead each quadrant's activity.

Close the loop. Even if you're not planning to publish your findings, it is nevertheless important to ensure that your results are evaluated and fed back into the next round of discussions. If possible, broadcast your findings to broader audiences, so others can use your findings.

5

ACT DIFFERENTLY

Connections among contributors

'Look at what connects and separates people.'
THE I CHING

Nearly every project I've been involved in that aims to address a complex problem relies on partnerships. Very often, my clients come to me with two complaints. Either they don't know who the right partners are, or if they do, they don't have enough influence to bring them to the table. As one senior executive in government put it, 'Andrew, I'm out of my depth when I don't have authority over my colleagues at my level in parallel agencies'.

Imagine for a moment the work of a typical government health department in your average modern Western democracy. They must plan (and often fund) basic health services like hospitals and clinics. They must attempt to protect the population from contaminated food and blood-borne viruses, promote research, and ensure that well-trained health professionals are in ongoing and adequate supply. Nowadays, with more sophisticated understandings of the social determinants of health, they may even get involved in preventing underlying causes such as joblessness, low educational attainment or poor housing. Depending on the economic system in which they operate, the department will regulate, provide incentives for private providers to do effective work (including insurers and researchers), train and educate people, distill data and information, and facilitate partnerships.

One of the most useful things a collective can do at the very outset of its work is to map the ecosystem of contributors to outcomes. In other words, visually display the power inter-relationships within your network. Ideally, such mapping needs to not only simplify the complex network of multi-level stakeholders, but illustrate the variations in their level of influence and importance. The relationships between contributors will also vary: funding from funders, representation by peak bodies, education from academics, coordination from other partner entities, and secondary consultation from advisory groups, such as consumer committees.

I usually advise clients working to solve complex social issues in partnership that they need to know three things, in this order:

1. in which sector your most useful partners reside, and *their priorities*
2. how important they are to your ability to achieve *your objectives*
3. the *degree of influence* you may assert on these potential partners

To look at how we might depict as a simple visual, let's revisit our example of a government health department. We know that a single regional office alone may have a hundred or more partner entities. These can be displayed on a diagram like the one opposite:

- Nine sectors equals nine shaded segments. Each sector's priorities can be recorded alongside.
- Three influence levels equals three concentric layers corresponding to the status of the partner. Are they are genuine partner with shared resources and objectives (and therefore an 'inner' partner) within your network? Are planning together and sharing some capacity building activities (middle) or are you merely within each other's ecosystems, meaning that you share information and remain aware of each other's activities (outer)?

Three things we must know about our co-contributors: sector, importance and influence

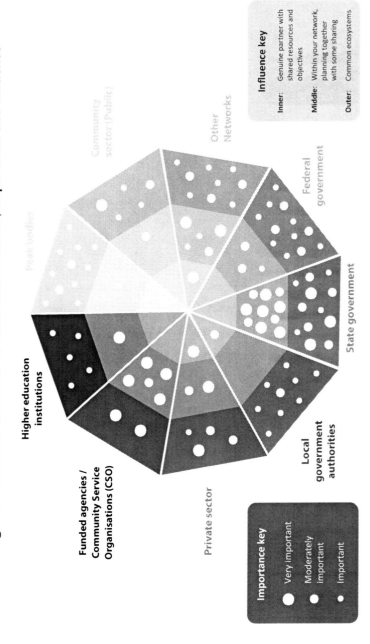

Higher education institutions

Funded agencies / Community Service Organisations (CSO)

Peak bodies

Community sector (Public)

Other Networks

Federal government

State government

Local government authorities

Private sector

Influence key

Inner: Genuine partner with shared resources and objectives

Middle: Within your network, planning together with some sharing

Outer: Common ecosystems

Importance key

⬤ Very important

● Moderately important

• Important

- Three levels of importance to achieving strategic objectives equals three dot sizes.

Such a diagram is diagnostically valuable for two reasons:

1. Investment of effort: You want a disproportionate level of partnership investment in two areas (inner circle with medium or large dots *and* middle circle with large dots). In the example here, this equates to a total of eighteen entities.

2. Identify strategic partnering risks: The more big dots you have in the outermost ring, the weaker your position is in that area. In other words, having a partner organisation on which you rely heavily to meet your strategic objectives, but with whom you have low levels of influence is a considerable strategic risk. In this example, this group comprises seven entities.

The dots do not necessarily have to represent individual agencies. They may be better conceived as representing a single logical connection at a strategic level. In other words, you are better off thinking of them as 'types' of stakeholders. A single private sector dot might represent, for example, general practitioners' (*not* Farnborough Medical Practice) or a single local government dot might by 'statutory planners', *not* an individual local government (in this case, the City of Farnborough). This also means that you limit the number of dots on your overall map. Having said that, you can if you wish do a separate map for the statutory planners for the twenty local government areas with which you interact, if the statutory planner dot is large enough.

In getting people to work together the power of a simple visual display can't be overestimated.

Key actions towards mapping contributions...

1. **Get the mapping question right**. Is the desired mapping based on geography, or sectors, or organisations, or people? Remember that the map should be diagnostic and address your most critical questions.

2. **Create a structure for the map that works**. While the boxes might contain an entity's name, what should the lines between them represent? What may their proximity imply? Keep it simple. A map that tries to do too many things will ultimately confuse people and defeat the purpose of the mapping exercise, which is to see at a glance the different types of contributions.

3. **Use the map**. Distribute it widely and often and use it for its diagnostic value. Update it and seek feedback from users.

6

ACT DIFFERENTLY

Interdependency and symbiotic effort

'Connect through your similarity and profit from your diversity.'

VALDIS KREBS & JUNE HOLLEY

Think about the last time you employed someone to do something for you — as a contractor, a vendor, or an employee. Vast and almost incomprehensible networks contributed to your ability to do this.

The US academic (and aspirant politician) Elizabeth Warren describes this complex social contract aptly: 'You built a factory out there? Good for you. But I want to be clear: you moved your goods to market on the roads the rest of us paid for; you hired workers the rest of us paid to educate; you were safe in your factory because of police forces and fire forces that the rest of us paid for. You didn't have to worry that marauding bands would come and seize everything at your factory, and hire someone to protect against this, because of the work the rest of us did.'[1]

Warren is right, but I'd go further: not only do we *use* these connections, we are all *products* of complex connections — and by virtue of being human, we *create even more* complex connections. But, how does this continuous interdependence happen? There are four notable features.

First, our social systems grew in complexity from our earliest history: we began living together in tribes and clans, then warrior-states and kingdoms, eventually moving to empires and nations, and now, increasingly, to alliances and unions. Each system has the ability to accommodate more and more people (tribal structures can comfortably accommodate 150 people, while economic unions such as the EU may boast 300 million members) but still retaining the integrity of *each person's* concerns, purposes and circumstances.

Without central control, each person nevertheless makes thousands of unsupervised decisions each day, and are often reliant on others to do so. From this reliance, we form 'organisations' with countless external and internal factors pressing and pulling. What is even more remarkable is that

---

[1] See http://www.youtube.com/watch?v=hOyDR2b71ag

these organisations have an innate tendency to maintain their integrity. Think about the ability of institutions to survive intact, such as the Catholic Church and giant Japanese business conglomerates such as Mitsubishi, which have been in existence for centuries.

Humans create interdependence in four ways, each with a separate motive force:

1. **Blind Interdependence**: This is when various component parts work independently but rely on each other. Think of the divisions of a traditional corporation, or an employment agency that places workers with firms. The motive force here is *rules*, ensuring that each party trades its resources equitably. Blind interdependence hones high levels of expertise and specialisation, but when it fails, it can do so spectacularly, because the rules don't account for unforeseen blowouts. A salient example here is General Motors' exposure to very high health and pension costs and its subsequent bankruptcy.

2. **Serial Interdependence**: Here the output of one part is the input of another, known to us in the assembly line, the supply chain and the electricity grid. A perfect example is the publishing industry that historically has linked writers, editors, agents, publishers, distributors and retailers in a linear fashion. The motive force here isn't rules,

Four types of interdependence

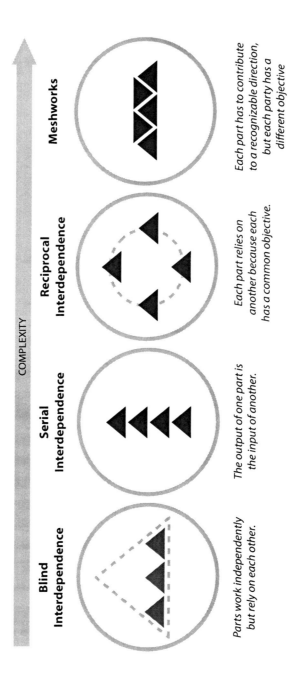

COMPLEXITY

Blind Interdependence

Parts work independently but rely on each other.

Serial Interdependence

The output of one part is the input of another.

Reciprocal Interdependence

Each part relies on another because each has a common objective.

Meshworks

Each part has to contribute to a recognizable direction, but each party has a different objective but *mediation*. Each part requires the ability to negotiate with the next, whether that's the simple negotiation of an assembly line component signaling it's ready to move on, or a publisher hammering out a deal with an author's agent. When failure occurs, it can be momentuous. Think of the blackouts on the USA Eastern Seaboard in 2010, the result of just a few defective parts of the grid shutting down.

3. **Reciprocal Interdependence**: This is when each part relies on another because each has a common objective. Typical examples are construction projects (with the need for the design, planning, technology and economics all to come together) and hospitals (where triage, staffing, beds, medicines, surgical units all require meticulous coordination). The motive force here is *feedback*, subjugating the natural state for individual determination.

4. **Meshworks**: These are the most complex interdependencies, where each part has to contribute to a recognisable direction, but each has a different objective. Road safety is a good example (with road builders, police, car designers and regulators tacitly coordinating one big outcome — safer roads — but each with different objectives) or infant mortality in developing nations (aid givers, medical personnel and educators). The motive force here is *iteration*: repeating parts of processes and learning from successive

approximations. This recognises an important feature of meshworks, absent from other types of interdependencies — that the process is emergent and the end-result will not be known at the outset.

Often, when things don't proceed as expected, it's the result of variable performance by partners, or of essential partners dropping out over time. The essential ingredient is not just to design collaborative work so that contributors are critically interdependent, but to understand the core nature of the task and whether the optimal form of interdependence sought is blind, serial or reciprocal — or a meshwork.

Key actions towards interdependence

If you're solving complex problems via a meshwork:

1. Start by eliminating turf warfare. You can't create a network where one element is acting against the interests of others. The key to resolve this is to use the motive force of the system that is 'simpler' than the one you are trying to create. For example, if you're interested in meshwork, then give feedback; if you want to create a useful serially interdependent system, establish rules.

2. Don't worry about critical mass; worry about the number of interconnections with a focus on which must be strong, and which can be weak (see Part 2, Chapter 5, Connections Amongst Contributors).

3. All interdependent systems have nodes or hubs, but establishing which are the most effective will maximise progress towards the goals you seek.

4. Don't get caught up in thinking about 'what' an organisation is (or what it isn't). Encourage your peers' to think about their work as increasingly porous and without boundaries. Do this by creating pools of resources in the form of 'virtual organisations' or by adopting new cross-organisational accountabilities.

Why this book is only the beginning

In the many thousands of hours I've spent working with groups on the mindset shifts and group actions in this book, I've observed three things about how people — eventually — come to agreement and clarity.

A. People invested in a solution aren't the best people to run the dialogue

- They are holders of power and others aren't comfortable tilting that balance
- They can't accurately gauge the balance of opinion that supports or opposes them
- They often become unhelpfully task-focused, pushing the group to conform with a pre-determined outcome
- They commit normal human errors of thinking (distortion, generalisation and sometimes, even total deletion) but often

fail to admit to (or even recognise) these.

B. People enmeshed in old ways of problem solving are those who most need new thinking tools

- People sometimes think they know 'the answer'. They do not. At best, they have *an* answer. At other times they have what I call 'premature understanding'.

- Someone with an independent view can provide a new frame, even without technical or specialist knowledge of the area concerned, because they understand *how to think about thinking* on the issue

- The most important thinking tool is the ability to 'chunk up' (*What is X an example of?*) and 'chunk down' (*What's an example of X?*), so that new relationships between ideas can be discovered.

C. The skills needed are neither conceptual nor interpersonal, they're both

- People often need to be shown that the major skill is not being able to solve a problem, but being able to ask the most potent questions.

- A vital group process is the ability to synthesise information without bias; this has both emotional and intellectual elements.

- The more complex the problem, the more important simplification is. The use of metaphor, stories or process visuals can help immeasurably in this regard.

- Experience helps a facilitator hone in on the most important elements within a range of views, even if they're conflicting, confusing or contradictory.

The real problem with a book like this is that it forces you to take in my thinking from a two-dimensional page, in a linear word-by-word, idea-by-idea fashion. If the technology existed, I'd present everything in these pages simultaneously. Why? Because solving the increasingly complex challenges of this century will require not just integrators, but multi-taskers who can balance several contradictory ideas in their heads at the same time, working on content while they're running a process, designing structures and systems while they're not sure of the outcome, and thinking about the outcome while they're uncertain about how to get there.

This tremendous simultaneity is the mark of the true integrator and, if you're one of them, I very much look forward to working with you one day.

CPSIA information can be obtained at www.ICGtesting.com
Printed in the USA
BVOW022231040413

317355BV00007B/34/P

9 780987 404800